HANNAH'S SHAME

Derek Leinster is a survivor. *Hannah's Shame* is the inspirational story of one boy's Irish childhood spent in poverty because of the neglect of the Church of Ireland, of his lifelong search for who he is and of his fight for justice. Abandoned by his birth mother in a Children's Home where illness, hunger and neglect were commonplace, fostered by an inordinately poor family and then living in poverty but ignored by the well-to-do community in which he was brought up, this is a story that will touch your heart. It is a story of shame.

HANNAH'S SHAME

HANNAH'S SHAME

by

Derek Leinster

Magna Large Print Books
Long Preston, North Yorkshire,
BD23 4ND, England.

British Library Cataloguing in Publication Data.

Leinster, Derek
    Hannah's shame.

    A catalogue record of this book is
    available from the British Library

    ISBN   978-0-7505-3438-3

First published in Great Britain in 2005 by Derek Leinster

Copyright © Derek Leinster

Cover illustration © Jill Battaglia by arrangement with
Arcangel Images

The moral right of the author has been asserted

Published in Large Print 2011 by arrangement with
Derek Linster

Magna Large Print is an imprint of Library Magna Books Ltd.

Printed and bound in Great Britain by
T.J. (International) Ltd., Cornwall, PL28 8RW

This book is based on my honest
recollections from my own life.

Some of the names have been changed,
to protect some people.

Acknowledgements

I've written this book with lots of help from Bernice Walmsley and would like to thank her for her hard work, her creative input and efficient organisation.

I'd also like to thank other people who helped me to realise the dream of writing a book about my life – Eva Rupp, Rita and all the ladies at the lay-by café known as Hot & Cold, Simon who played his own part and the many others, too numerous to mention, who have made a valuable, and valued, contribution in the process of bringing this book together.

Above all, I must thank my wife for putting up with hearing about this story continuously over many, many years and my four daughters – Debbie, Amanda, Gail and Kerry – who have also had to endure this marathon.

Derek Leinster 2005

Where are they?

I need to know where they are, I cannot hear them, I cannot see them, where would they be?
Are they here, are they there? I cannot see them anywhere.
Where have they gone? I am worried.
I cannot bear it, I am alone.
Are they here, are they there? I cannot see them anywhere.
Let me know if you spot them, for I cannot see where they are.
I do not know them properly yet, I would love to get to know them.
MUM, DAD please appear!

Hannah Summers
Derek's granddaughter
(10 years old)

Notes re Derek Linster from Canon Stanley Baird

I was instituted as Rector of the Parish of Dunganstown in Co. Wicklow in 1959. The Rectory was a short distance from the parish National School. Artie Donald, who was Sexton of the Parish Church lived, along with his family, in an old, rather run-down cottage adjacent to the school. He was a widower and not very domesticated. Conditions in the house would not have been the best. Two unmarried aunts of Artie, May and Daisy, lived nearby. They were rather unusual and regarded as 'characters' locally. I imagine that neither Artie nor his aunts had very much money to meet their needs.

Soon after I arrived Derek came to see me. I had already got the impression that he was different from the rest of the family. He was intent on joining the British Army and required a character reference from me. I believe that I gave him the reference glad to discover that he had ambition and wanted to make 'something' of his life. I felt that if he remained in the environment of his home in Dunganstown that it would be difficult to develop his full potential.

When I met Derek I did not know that he was a foster child, believing that he was adopted. However, in the course of providing him with a reference we discovered that this was not so and that his correct surname was Linster. As this was his legal name I advised him to use it in future. I imagine that I referred to him in the reference as Derek Linster. He was not accepted into the army on the grounds of age.

Shortly after this Artie and his family left the district and my contact with them and with Derek came to an end.

I am now glad to know that Derek made a success of his life and that he is planning to produce in book from the story of his life. I wish him and this venture every success and I look forward to reading his story in due course.

Foreword

My story is different from most, yet many similar strands that ran through my Protestant, poverty-stricken existence as a child are mirrored in the experiences of others. They have shared the same pain and suffering. However, there are some important – and sometimes startling – differences. Unlike many in Ireland at the time, I was not born to poverty. My parents were from relatively well-off backgrounds. They had cars, businesses and property. They led comfortable, well-fed lives.

So why did I grow up in total poverty? The reason I had to grow up impoverished and totally abused through the lack of care bestowed upon me was because of religious dogma and for no other reason than that.

The purpose of my story is to make a testament to the years I lost because of the pure hypocrisy that was so prominent in Irish society in my early years. In this story

I cover the pain, the suffering and the shame that I – and many others – were forced to endure. However, my recollections are framed in humour and irony, which is odd when you consider the hopelessness of my case, and my position as a young child and then as a young boy growing up in Ireland. As a young person, I was totally abandoned by all authority, by all of those who were supposed to care for children and by the government. My own church, the Church of Ireland, also deserted me – so I was totally alone.

It is important to note here that usually at this time in Ireland – the mid twentieth century – the poverty-stricken conditions that I was raised in and the pain and suffering I endured were not usually considered to apply to Protestant children like me. Most people in those particular circumstances would have been Catholic. They would have been born into poverty and remained there. Abandoned Catholic children also suffered total rejection. But in my case I was raised a Protestant and had not started my life in poverty-stricken circumstances. Both of my parents were very reasonably off during 1940s Ireland. But I was not to benefit from this fortunate set of circumstances.

Throughout my childhood, Ireland had always portrayed herself as a very, very religious and God-fearing country. This representation is at odds with the cruelty I experienced during my younger years and the experiences of all those other lost souls and hopeless causes who were raised within the heart of this supposedly Christian country.

The concept of abuse within the Catholic Church in Ireland is, of course, well documented. Even the Taoiseach (The Irish Prime Minister) himself – Bertie Ahern – on behalf of the state of Ireland, made a public apology to former victims of the institutional Catholic school system. However, the Church of Ireland has been far more successful at covering up the skeletons in her closet. Perhaps this is because the Church of Ireland was hugely influenced by snobbery. Or perhaps it is simply because Ireland is perceived to be a Catholic domain and all other denominations, without that weight of numbers, are ignored, bypassed and generally hidden. The Catholic Church in Ireland has had a special relationship with the state, which is enshrined within the constitution. Perhaps the impact of this rendered those of us who were raised within the care of the Church of Ireland as invisible. I would not wish to suggest that the Catholic

Church were not adept at hiding abuse – don't get me wrong, the Catholics also covered it up. However, it is my firm belief that they were not as professional and skilful as the Church of Ireland were at this game.

As for my story, I was one of the rare ones that managed to defy the church, to overcome the obstacles that the Church of Ireland and the authorities put in my way and to succeed where so many others before and after failed. Against all the odds I did it, I discovered who I was. After all, everyone needs to know what he or she is and from where they came. Identity is so important and so central to a person's sense of being.

It is paramount that we, as survivors, are able to make some sense out of the turmoil of our lives and out of the total lack of knowing what on earth we are about, and out of how we landed on this earth without any normal family connections. In doing so we uncover the truth of our very existence. I want and hope that I may be able to hold a ray of light for those who have lived my experience to follow, to realise that they should never give up the pursuit of tracking down and ending the mystery, wherever they may be.

I suppose a lot of people might want to

know why anybody would want to write a book of this nature. My answer is simple. I feel I must submit this testament, as a survivor of the hell that I was forced to endure and because of the hypocrisy of the religious community and the nonsense that was inflicted onto all of us. I want to document history for those who did not make it through to adulthood, as there are many unwanted children who did not survive the ordeal. In their memory and for all of us who lived and are still searching for what was taken away, I dedicate this book.

My testament should read like a long diary, where I have managed to record the events of my life. This is my story.

Chapter 1

My story begins

I began life in 1941 when I was born to people who were well off. My mother's family were well-to-do Protestant farmers and my father's people were also in business. Although some of them may have thought that they were having a hard time, to me, growing up, surrounded by the same kind of people, they appeared far from poor. In those days people experiencing total poverty were certainly not able to drive around in cars and did not own farms and garages. Poor people were not dressed in good quality clothes. They didn't take plentiful food for granted. I suppose my parents, by comparison, had to be an awful lot better off than a great many other people.

My upbringing was in complete contrast to this background. I spent most of my childhood dressed in rags and hungry. I could only dream about a life where there was enough to eat and where affection and care was taken for granted. My parents' wealth did not touch my life.

My father was a big man – well over 6 feet tall and in his prime would have weighed over 18 stones. I've been told that he had spent a short spell in the local police force and, in fact, they provided a guard of honour at his funeral so he was obviously well respected. Following a falling out with his brother who had originally set him up in business with money he had made in America before the stock market crash, he took over the garage in Drumconrath from about 1937–38 and worked extremely hard to build up a thriving business. It was coming to the end of an era where everything was done by horses so you could imagine the dedication, hard work and knowledge that would be necessary. Society had started to change and you really had to have very sound judgement when, for example, somebody was trading in his or her horses to buy a tractor. It is these sorts of decisions that could very quickly bankrupt a business if you didn't have a sharp eye on the changes that were unfolding at a very fast pace. And don't forget that this was in a country that had hardly put its head up out of the dark ages in terms of new technology. When my father was working hard to establish his business it was also a time of great upheaval in the world and in Ireland in particular. It wasn't long since the first world war had ended and Ireland had had its own war of independence and then their own internal war following the war of home rule where you had brother against brother, father against son – normally the bitterest conflict of all. Evidently, all of this mayhem kept Ireland a good hundred years behind the times. So, anyone who could make a success of his business during this period would have been nobody's fool.

To illustrate what a success my father made of this business, you should know that he was driving one of those big old Singer cars around when most people had difficulty in affording a donkey or a pushbike – and this on top of raising nine children!

My parents were not married. My father was Catholic and had been insistent that I was to be raised as a Catholic. It was invariably expected that any child born to a Catholic during that time was going to be raised as Catholic. There was no discussion on the matter. It was just a fact of life at that time and in that place. My mother Hannah's family were, however, fiercely Protestant, and would under no circumstances tolerate me being raised as a Catholic. Stalemate. So rather than endure the indignity of having me raised as a Catholic my mother's family had me sent away and expelled from the family. I was banished from the very existence of my being all because of snobbery, bigotry and saving face.

Simply being wrenched from one's family and plunged into poverty was bad enough, but there were yet more wrongs to be done to babies like me in the name of the church. Children born to families of unmarried mothers who were subsequently taken into care often had their names changed and their identities removed to ensure that the scandal of their illegitimacy (and in my case, the religious problem) was minimised. Furthermore the church would go to any lengths to make sure that such offspring could never find their way back home or search out their family members.

My story will tell how I was fostered to a family who could hardly take care of themselves – and certainly could not offer a good home to a defenceless child. And it will also tell how this debacle, that was to affect me so awfully in childhood and for the rest of my life, was arranged and sanctioned by officials working for the Church of Ireland. My health suffered from babyhood to the present day. My education was non-existent and, of course, this has affected me throughout my life. In childhood I was habitually referred to as 'the poor eejit' and in adulthood I was unable to apply for the jobs that I felt sure I could do. The lack of love and affection that I experienced must surely have affected me mentally and emotionally. And, above all, I was deeply affected by not knowing my background and this has become a lifelong quest for me – to find out who I am.

During my childhood, I lived among the parishioners of the Church of Ireland but I doubt that they would believe that such utter deprivation and cruelty was present within their own people or that the children of their church were subjected to this most horrendous existence. Although I am sure that they would readily agree that such atrocities occurred within the scope of the Catholic Church, the idea of accepting that a very real abuse of power was present within their own church would be unthinkable. The idea to me that Protestant children who were in care would be treated better than their Catholic counterparts purely because of the Protestant doctrine seems utterly ridiculous and I really don't understand why so many people believed this to be so.

Whatever their reasons, this was certainly not the case and that is why I feel it is important for this story to be told. I want to expose the myths and the hypocrisy that surrounded the Church of Ireland. Religion did not make a difference in the amount of suffering imposed on the children in this situation – it just meant that one religion acknowledged the problem and the other ignored it even when it was in front of their eyes on a daily basis.

In complete contrast to the Catholic Church, the Church of Ireland has never accepted any responsibility for destroying children's lives. The hierarchy of the Protestant church in Ireland was somehow always protected. In my case, an experience in recent years served to remind me of the lack of value placed on our lives as children. When I was trying to acquire information about my personal history at the Church of Ireland Records Section, the woman behind the counter informed me, with an icy calm, that the church would not wish to have records about me, or about anybody who was raised in similar circumstances. Furthermore, and perhaps by way of explanation for this apparent oversight in the records office, she seemed quite happy to remind me that there was more value put on the muck on the bottom of my mother's shoes and those of her family who came into the office at the Bethany Home in 1941 than the value that there would have been put on me as a person. That is essentially how unimportant we were! We children of the Church of Ireland who were adopted and fostered were so unimportant that officially we do not exist.

Of course not all of the children who were dumped into the care of the Church of Ireland had the same experience that I had. Some were certainly well looked after and I was to see for myself an example of this. The war refugees that the Government took in during, and at the end of, the war were not neglected as I was. Those refugees' affairs were organised by the Red Cross who insisted that these children could not be discharged into an Irish Free State institution. They insisted instead that families would foster them, as they obviously did not trust the institutions to give them the care they needed. I attended school with one of these refugee children and he seemed like a millionaire to me. I was ashamed to be near him because of my wretched condition and the state of my clothes, but there was no doubt that he was well looked after. It seemed a pity to me that some of this attention was not administered to children like myself as well as the refugee babies. But, as I was to realise later, the Red Cross took their responsibilities far more seriously than did the Church of Ireland.

In 1941, the world was tearing itself apart in the Second World War, but isn't it strange that amongst all of this mayhem, people's daily habits and instincts do not change one little bit? They still carry on in their normal, haphazard ways, as if none of this mayhem existed. And none more so than the people who lived in the little, sleepy village of Drumconrath, Co. Meath, where my mother's family farmed and my father ran his garage and his farm. Their families were good neighbours to each other. My mother's people had their old wireless batteries charged at my father's garage and many of the relatives on my mother's side would have bought their vehicles there, insured them through him and had them repaired there too, as his garage had the main dealership for Roote's motor company in that area. As a teenager Hannah, my mother, who was about ten years younger than my father and was no doubt flattered at the attentions of this successful businessman, used to have her punctures on her bicycle repaired at his garage, but then old human nature spun into action and my mother and father turned to fancy each other as human nature dictates. But in these cases life can take a twist that neither party had bargained for. Yes, you've guessed it; a baby was on the way. Even under normal circumstances this would be very bad news, but in the situation that existed between the two families regarding religion it was a totally different affair – a disaster. In those days in Ireland, where Protestants and Catholics got on well together in all other aspects of life, things would change totally if there were marriages considered between them or babies born before going through a wedding ceremony. The Catholic Church held a totally non-negotiable position on children. As I have already said, they would insist that any child born to a Catholic family – irrespective of the other family's religion – would have to be brought up as a Catholic. This created a situation where thousands of children were to become unwanted and uncared for. Like the Catholic church, the Church of Ireland had its own stubbornness and snobbery so this meant that in a situation like the one my parents found themselves in it was like throwing petrol on a fire that is already out of control.

In the years before the war, many Church of Ireland girls who found themselves in this sort of position would have gone over to England to obtain an illegal abortion. But while the war was going on, the danger from U-boats meant that few people travelled across the Irish Sea, So many more Protestant babies were born out of wedlock during the war years. The war made little or no difference in this respect to the Catholic girls who became pregnant outside wedlock as their religion would not countenance abortion so that wasn't an option for them. Of course, this meant that there were always more Catholic babies born and more Catholic orphanages in existence to cater for them.

So this is where my story starts. At four and a half months old my mother, Hannah, left me at the orphanage. I have often wondered what was in her mind as she walked away from me that day. Did she have any regrets? Did she worry about the tiny baby she was leaving behind? She is now nearly eighty years of age. She obviously has had a hard road to travel in her life to get where she is today, but I doubt if there was any bigger an obstacle to overcome on her life's journey than the one she dealt with on that particular day.

Chapter 2

Leaving the 'hell-hole'

Outside the Bethany Home in Rathgar, Dublin, where my mother had been sent as an unmarried mother-to-be in the early 1940s, the Second World War was raging, but inside the Home battles of a far more personal nature were being fought and disasters happened on a daily basis to the people supposedly being cared for there. And this is where I was condemned to start my life.

In the early part of the twentieth century, before its owners fell on hard times because demand for private education for middle-class Protestants had fallen away, the Bethany Home had been a private boarding school. But by 1940, this once-grand Georgian style house had been converted into an orphanage run by the Church of Ireland. The décor and furnishings would have been very basic and faded by the time I arrived at the Bethany Home but originally it would have been a place of grandeur, with polished wood panelling and probably crystal chandeliers.

From the day the children of the pious Christians of the Church of Ireland were dumped in the orphanages they essentially fended for themselves. No specific person ever seemed responsible for checking on them to ensure that they thrived, certainly not the State or the higher echelons of the church carried out this task anyway. So it appeared to me, at least, that nobody knew, beyond the boundary of the orphanage walls, what was being done – or not being done – in the interest of childcare, health and educational backup. Many of these children were damaged severely and permanently by the horrendous experience that they encountered in their very young lives. This continued even when they left the Home, when children were dumped with foster families who were already struggling with everyday life and had no interest in making sure that health and educational provision were factors in these children's lives. To be fair, the families who took children in, were offered no support or assistance themselves. This meant that many of these children had to overcome their daily nightmares alone. It is a fact widely acknowledged that any child who endures this kind of horrific treatment, with constant upheavals and without love, care or attention, only stigmatised as a problem or burden, would inevitably be prone to poor mental health and low self-esteem throughout their lives.

The conditions in the Bethany Home are something that could best be described as hellish. In this hole of inexplicable horror abandoned babies – like me – were placed. Babies and toddlers were, in effect, abandoned. Food was basic – barely enough to keep them alive. They were left for hour after miserable hour with nothing to eat or drink, unchanged nappies, unwiped noses and, of course, the mental stimulation was non-existent. In short, no one gave them any care or attention – and certainly no love. Even the very basic care ceased for me when I was only a few months old. My mother, who had been made to take care of me (in addition to her cleaning duties in the Home) as a form of punishment for her sin of getting pregnant outside the sanctity of marriage, left the Home and went back to her life among her family. Then the lottery-like care given by the staff in the Home swung into action. The losers in this lottery, of course, were always the children. The memory of their sullen eyes and ashen faces, with the smell of death all around, will remain with me forever. The experience of the orphanage was something that would haunt a normal human being until the day they died. My mother, who I was to meet many years later, herself described Bethany as a 'hellhole'. She had been relieved to leave and had never looked back.

Apart from the appalling lack of care and attention that was shown to the children in the Bethany Home, there were many rumours about even more serious issues. These babies and infants would scream uncontrollably because of their wretched condition. They would cry for food and for the basic necessity of human contact. It was said that those who looked after us in the orphanage became so frustrated by the pitiful, hungry cries of the babies and small children there that they resorted to holding a pillow over the baby's face – until the crying stopped and death had taken over. I am unable to prove that this actually happened of course, but I certainly believe that if an adult human being could allow a defenceless infant to lie in soiled nappies, unwashed and unfed to a point where they were half dead, then it is certainly conceivable to kill them so they no longer had to listen to their cries. Some of the people who were quite closely involved with the Bethany Home at that time firmly believe that this did take place. Ironically many of these unwanted babies born to Church of Ireland families would have been the finest and healthiest babies born in Ireland, because their parents came from some of the more privileged backgrounds in the country. For these people to allow infants to end up in such chronic sickness simply to protect the reputations and family names within the Church of Ireland is indicative of how rotten middle-class Irish society was at its heart. As a culture, members acted out the myth that they were somehow better, more holy and more devout than those who practiced other faiths.

You see, when you go into all of this, you find the churches and the governments are the real causes of having their people be so ashamed. The dread of the loss of face and the fear of losing their worthless family pride has been created by these organisations. There should be no shame in having children whether married or unmarried. That's just a man-made illusion, but in actual fact where there is shame – real shame – in having children in or out of marriage is when you dump them for someone else to look after. That's when real shame kicks in. What we should be doing is creating a society that makes people recognize their responsibility for caring, without question, for the ones that they have brought into this world. It is so frustrating to me that the solution should be so simple. The pompous nonsense associated with religion and family names should have been spotted, acknowledged and eradicated. That's where thousands of people would have been saved the injustice and suffering that they were made to endure. And this was all so that the powers-that-be could pretend to the world that they had not a blemish on their souls. So that they could be an example to be held up for all good thinking new generations to aspire to and then they could pretend that the responsibilities that they failed to fulfil didn't exist. The abandoned and damaged children could be something that they could put to the back of their minds and they could pretend for the rest of their lives that all of this didn't really happen, just so they could live at ease amongst their fellow pretenders. The effect was that the local community had a totally wrong picture of the real situation. Of course, in this society of pretence there are no winners because all sides become victims, the child, the mother and sometimes the fathers as well, as their families will always have their hidden shame

A few months after my mother had left the home, when I was seven and half months old, my life was to be drastically changed yet again. A local woman, Mrs Trainer, who had experienced the real but hidden horror of the orphanages and had been left with an impression she could never forget, fostered me for a time. Mrs Trainer bestowed warmth and kindness upon me and all the other children she took away from the home. She was light in the darkness of our world, she fostered children to give them some hope and an escape from the pit of hell known as The Bethany Home. I feel now as an adult that simply because of the effort she made to care for us, I owe her my best endeavours to prevent such places as the Bethany Home ever being tolerated again.

Chapter 3

Happier Times and Back to the Start

At the age of 7½ months one of the happiest periods of my childhood started when I was fostered to a family in Nuns Cross, Co. Wicklow. I arrived at the Trainers' farmhouse on a cold January day, wrapped only in a white shawl. My head was a mass of scabs, pus and blood. I have been told since that my foster family purchased some cream from a pharmacy some 4 or 5 miles away. To this day I have never discovered what sort of cream it was, but nevertheless the son of my new foster mother used to rub the cream into my head and it obviously did the trick as I was well known for my big, bushy, chestnut-coloured hair.

So this is where my story starts, at the Trainer's farm at Nuns Cross at 7½ months old. It was a mixed farm – some cows, some sheep and so on – with a lovely old farmhouse that was typical of the area. I grew up mostly in the care of Tom Trainer, the son of the lady who fostered me – Mrs Trainer. She had been married three times apparently, probably because of the early deaths of her husbands. Deaths and remarriages were extremely common in those days as people often worked hard and died young. Women especially died prematurely – mostly during childbirth. I only learnt all this recently during my search for my childhood – a task that has taken me almost all of 50 years now.

My new foster mother was one of the very few adults I ever knew who saw and acknowledged the suffering that children endured in the Church of Ireland orphanages. Because she had seen the conditions that the abandoned children were being raised in, she tried to save some of them by offering an escape from the Bethany Home. Mrs Trainer was obviously very concerned about the state of these unwanted infants. After being introduced to the home by a friend so that she could have personal viewing of the gross neglect that was being served up in the name of civilization and of Christianity, she couldn't help being profoundly shocked. She had the images of these helpless children engraved in her mind; images that were to haunt her for the rest of her life. She was so moved by what she saw that she started to take the children to look after personally. As she was a busy farmer you can imagine how deep her desire to care for these children must have been. With all of her other commitments in her very busy life (and as she was a woman in her 50's) it certainly wasn't the best time to be loading herself up with very small children. She took on all the tasks – having to worry about toilet training and getting the children to walk – when she was already overworked on the farm, simply because she was so moved and so outraged with a society that she had looked up to and respected.

All the children that I remember whom she brought to the house had experienced a horrendous, unspeakable deficiency in human care to such an extent that they looked like the dead brought back to life. It saddens me now to think that I too must have been one of these barely-alive children – children who were not afforded even the very basic nutrition, cleanliness or care. Often they were left in soiled nappies, unwashed and only fed occasionally. Is it any wonder that we were riddled with disease? All of the poor children that she rescued from the Bethany Home were in a dreadful state beyond words. Many had open sores all over their bodies – sores that were rarely attended to while they were in the Home, so they just got worse. All were poorly clothed and so badly fed that they were suffering from the effects of malnutrition. One of the most difficult aspects of the treatment these children were subjected to at the Bethany Home was the lack of love and affection. This could affect each child in different ways. Some were quiet and withdrawn while others were noisy and out of control. All were damaged by it. All of this was done in the name of God and the love of God and religion and it certainly makes you wonder where the people in charge of the home and the authorities who allowed this lack of care to go on were coming from.

I suppose I would have had a happy couple of years with the Trainers. The family were pig farmers and very busy people. Poor old Tom, who was all of nine years old, certainly drew the short straw by having to look after me. His mother had looked after many children and was also looking after other children from the Bethany Home.

Tom used to take me down with the cows to graze the long acre. To think that in those days they were doing the long acre on the main Dublin to Wexford road! The long acre refers to the strip of land alongside the road where people who owned just a few cattle or sheep could take them to graze for free. Taking the animals there was usually a job for the children of the family before and after school. This gives you some idea of how the traffic situation has changed. These days that old road is no longer used and there's a big by-pass to get you from Dublin to Wexford. Now it's even going to be turned into a motorway all the way to Wexford with cars going by as quickly as you can blink! However, in those days there were just cows grazing at the side of the roadways and eating the lush grass. Sometimes, Tom would take me down to the little brook where I used to take my shoes off and paddle in the water. He would also take me to the big oak tree that stood in the middle of where the road forked. This huge oak tree had a little seat in it that grew out of the bark. I remember he used to place me there while he tended to the cattle. I was happy there, with the sun shining on me, with no traffic tearing past – only the bliss of quietness and peace surrounded that scene in those long gone days. We did not worry about the danger of skin cancer to young skin because, in those days, it was unheard of. Tom reckoned that when he met me I was a terror, always wanting to be off into the gardens and to my favourite spots. He would tell me tales of what could happen to me if I wandered off but, of course, I didn't listen. He had a particular horror of a 60ft-deep well in the garden and warned me many, many times not to go near it. However, I didn't keep away. I wouldn't be satisfied until I was heading up to this well to have a good look at it, of course. Now, as I was only a toddler that wasn't a good idea but that's what being a child is about – going somewhere you shouldn't be going.

Tom has since told me about the old wheelbarrow which he used to take me up and down the fields in. It was a handsome barrow – handmade by a local blacksmith. One day he had me in the barrow, wheeling me up and down the farmyard with me squealing with excitement, and the barrow tipped over near the yard gate. I crashed out of it and cut my lip on the gate. There was blood everywhere and poor old Tom got a hiding for his antics with the barrow. Funnily enough, Tom has recently very kindly given me that old wheelbarrow which I now have in a prime position in my garden – fully done up and it looks wonderful, even though it's getting on for a hundred years old.

I stayed with the Trainers until I was about 2½ years old and then one morning a car arrived and took me and another little boy – Sam – back to the Bethany Home. Incidentally poor old Sam seems to have disappeared without trace. The Trainers never heard another word from him and nobody knows what happened to him. It would be great to hear from Sam who was fostered to the Trainer family in Nun's Cross in Co. Wicklow, the garden of Ireland. There was no explanation given for our sudden move and I have never found out the reason why we were taken forcibly from the Trainer family. It couldn't have been because of bad treatment because you couldn't possibly get treatment that was any worse than the place I was going to.

Mrs Trainer had been campaigning to have a stop put to the suffering of unwanted babies although she must surely have known the response she would get to her protests. She was simply unable to stand silently by when this unbelievable truth was exposed to her when she visited the Bethany Home. For her trouble she was, in the end, persecuted by those who wanted to pretend there was no such thing happening in their organisation. It is for this reason that I believe she was banished from having these children – so that the powers-that-be could continue to pretend that everything in the garden was lovely. There can be no doubt that the governing body responsible for the Bethany Home was not best pleased with her outcry and the trouble that she caused. But why we were all grabbed and taken away from Mrs Trainer's home with such haste, I have never discovered.

I do not know all of the facts surrounding this surprising snatching of us but in my case there may also have been another factor. My mother had made occasional visits to see me whilst I was at the Trainers'. This may have caused her mother – my grandmother – some concern as she would no doubt have wanted my mother to sever all contact with me. Perhaps her plan was to get me away to another family where my mother could not find me. It could also have been that my father was getting closer to finding my whereabouts so that he could have raised me as he had wished to do. This is guesswork of course as I don't know the full 'ins and outs' of these facts. I have to accept that I probably never will know all the facts as my mother holds the key to resolving this mystery.

I wasn't long back at the Bethany Home when I got all four of the terrible children's diseases of the time – Pertussis (Whooping Cough), Bronchial Pneumonia, Diphtheria and Enteritis – any one of which would normally have killed an infant or a young child. I went through that for 4½ months at the Cork Street Isolation Hospital (The Recovery and Fever Hospital Cork Street Dublin 8). Of course, being from the Bethany Home meant that, as a three year old in an isolation ward in hospital, I had nobody at all visiting me. Apart from hospital staff, there was nobody on the earth that would have given a damn as to whether I lived or died. If they were telling my mother and her people anything at all, the sky pilots (religious extremists) with whom my mother's family dealt would be telling them, I have no doubt, that this was God's way of solving the problem for them. They might have added that I would be better off going to heaven. They certainly would not have bargained for the wonderful nursing staff and doctors that were at the Cork Street hospital. These marvellous staff probably hadn't read their script and their only concern was to do everything they could to make a young, defenceless child survive.

From what was almost an impossible situation, and through their efforts and the grace of God I survived. Little by little I fought off each of the illnesses and, under the care of the nurses, gained strength and weight. My survival however, only meant that I eventually returned to the nightmare that was the Bethany Home in Dublin and back to more treatment that would affect my health.

This episode helps the picture to start to come into focus. Once you begin scratching away at the coating of secrecy, what you find is not very pleasant. It is obvious that they had good reasons to instil a clandestine culture. The treatment and lack of care that I would have had to receive at the Home to end up in such a pitiful state of health, within a short space of time back there, must have been horrendous. Medical experts here in England contend that for a child to become so ill you would have to be placed in a manure heap and to be abandoned – I suppose that just about sums up the Bethany Home!

After my return to the Home following my long stay in hospital, I was very hastily fostered out to a family in Dunganstown, Co. Wicklow by the name of Donald. Unfortunately for me, the family that was fostering me was unable to care even for themselves. They weren't just poor; they were destitute and would, under normal circumstances, never have been given the responsibility for another baby. They had just lost a son through pneumonia and my new foster mother became pregnant again whilst they were going through with my adoption. I say 'adoption', but I should note here that they were actually going through fostering arrangements rather than an adoption because there wasn't a legal adoption system in Ireland until after 1952. However, as far as they were concerned I was adopted. The adoption papers were a complete joke. I have since obtained copies of these papers and when you read them you would think that whoever compiled them was completely on the binge for weeks drinking nothing but Pocheen, as they made no sense at all. There was plenty of gibberish contained in the documents, but funnily enough there was one clear piece in them. This stated that I had to be adopted by a Protestant family – it was compulsory. It appeared that it didn't matter whether I was being looked after properly or not, but I had to be adopted by a Protestant family. That will give you some idea of what a horribly inhuman, unthinking policy was being acted out through the churches and will tell you just where their priorities lay. I have to make it very clear that the people who fostered me (the Donalds) were not bad people – they were just incompetent. My foster father seemed unable to hold a job down for long and my foster mother had enough problems looking after the child she had and the one she was expecting without taking on even more work. They were incapable of looking after themselves, never mind having to look after a child who had been through what I had been through – a child who obviously was very badly effected by its past. The Church of Ireland home should have made sure that whomever they chose to look after me was able to fully consider all my needs. To this day I do not understand why the authorities did not take their duties and responsibilities seriously. They should have checked up to make sure that everything was done correctly with follow-up visits and maybe some help for the struggling foster family, but of course that did not happen. I was just dumped with this inadequate foster family and was, seemingly, of no further concern to the Church of Ireland.

You have to take on board that no matter

how awful the conditions were for children whose lives were ruined by religious organizations, the people of Ireland were not like that by nature in terms of being cruel, uncaring or brutal. The ordinary people were wonderful. Do you know of anywhere else where you can go and ask somebody the way when you are lost and they'll tell you the direction and then call you in and give you a meal? I haven't come across it much in my life but you will certainly find that in many places in rural Ireland. However, in Co. Meath at that time I was soon to find out that it was a place that was completely different, a place where the religious extremists seemed to have taken hold.

Chapter 4

Being Fostered

When I arrived to start life with my new foster family in Dunganstown as a four year old I was relatively well dressed (I even had a waistcoat, although I was soon to discover that my new life would not call for much dressing up!) and spoke with what the locals believed to be a very posh accent. They would deliberately entice me to speak – just to hear me go on I suppose. The accent that I had is a bit of a mystery. I can only attribute it, with hindsight, to the attention I received, while I was with the Trainers, from Mrs Trainer's brother who, I believe, was a pretty well-educated person. The new clothes were the last lot I ever received as a child. It seemed to be accepted practice with these Church organizations that when they were dumping the kids they would make sure that they were in new clothes. Maybe they were desperate to make a good impression – something that was always part of the psyche of these people. Or maybe they knew the poverty-stricken plight that they were placing me in so it was their way of preparing me for what I was about to face. I suppose that it made them feel good that I had the new clothes. And maybe they would have thought that this one act of humanity – the only one of which I was conscious from them in my entire life – would be a big help to them in the life hereafter. I now wonder to myself that surely they couldn't have reckoned that these clothes would last me my whole childhood till I was able to earn my own keep, so where did they think I would get my next set of clothes?

My new foster family comprised of my foster father, Arthur Donald, who was a competent herdsman and often tried his hand at other jobs too but had real difficulty in holding down any job for very long, plus my foster mother who was pregnant when I arrived. There was one daughter at the time – Molly, who was almost a year older than me – but they had just lost a son to pneumonia and another baby was on the way. Because of this the situation soon changed from my being a wanted new son to being surplus to requirements. There was little space for me in the crowded, poorly furnished house but, to be fair to them, they put up with me. I suppose the best way to describe it would be that I was like a pet dog – you feed it when you have food and you give it water if you have it. That was the way I was treated and when they didn't have it they didn't give it to me. They would, however, always like to see the old dog in the shed irrespective of what the current situation might be. It is very difficult to explain this, it was a strange situation because normally if a family can't deal with something like this they would ask for help or they would take the child back. You would certainly do something – but that didn't happen in my case. I went through all of this mess and, as I obviously can't mind read, I can't give the answers as to why it happened as it did. All I can do by way of explanation is to outline what my experiences were and have been since the day I arrived at my foster parents' home.

Arthur Donald was born to a family in Dublin and at the time his father worked for Guinness. As you may or may not know, in the period prior to 1914, that wasn't a bad job to have so they presumably had a comfortable existence. For Arthur this didn't continue for long as his mother died when he was only six months old. His grandmother, Mrs Reynolds (owner of the hill house, Dunganstown) raised him. He had two brothers who were in the Canadian Army and as the Great War had just broken out, in 1914, they were obviously involved and were both killed, relatively close together, in France. Arthur's father was so distraught, so frustrated by losing his wife and two of his sons in quick succession that he joined the British Army and he himself was killed inside the first week of being in France. So, from there on in Arthur Donald – who was to become my foster father – was raised on a hill farm in Dunganstown, Co. Wicklow instead of on some estate in Dublin. Although he obviously had a very sad start to his life, Arthur was very, very lucky that his grandmother was raising him because she was unique – a wonderful woman. There are very few people on God's earth that will ever come up to her standards in terms of her efficiency and competence and also in her goodness as not only did she take responsibility for her grandson but she also raised several families who were orphaned due to the sinking of the Titanic in 1912.

Arthur would have been about 5'9" in height and very well-built and he always seemed to me to be a very strong person. He had blue eyes and the highly coloured, countrified complexion that picked him out as not belonging to the gentry but as someone who spent a lot of time outdoors. He usually wore a brown trilby hat and always seemed to be smoking – either cigarettes or a pipe. During the week he would just wear ordinary flannel trousers and a tweed jacket and he would have a suit of clothes for 'Sunday best'. All his clothes would have been many years old. In character, he was someone who would always have to be the best at what he was doing and if he couldn't achieve that he would take no part in that activity. He was very well equipped to be at the head of his gang, as you might say, because he was quite outgoing, well-liked. I remember that he had a bicycle for transport but when he went to the pub more often than not he would get one of his mates to put it in the boot of their car and take him home in their car. His cronies would have had no reason not to respect him – he certainly wasn't a rogue and was not into crime, so he would have been known as a good character. Of course, if he had worked regularly then things would have been very different for him, for his family and for me.

Kathleen Donald, my foster mother, had long black hair, usually with hair clips holding it in place but sometimes – when she was out in Daisy's field for instance – she would also use bits of cloth as ribbons in her hair. Whatever she did to decorate it or to hold it back, her hairstyle was one that could make the worse possible impression on people. It certainly couldn't be considered stylish. She was a gaunt figure, bespectacled, pale faced, with an air of sadness and hopelessness around her. With her thin figure and lank black hair she never looked, as you might say, 'in the pink'. The clothes she wore didn't help either. Her footwear would have seen better days and her clothes were always someone else's throwaways. They very rarely fitted her properly but she didn't seem to care. Despite the grind of her life and her worn down look she still had the will to carry out God's work in assisting the Church of Ireland Missionary.

Of course, Kathleen was a victim of the religious madness that was pushed down the Irish people's throats. Apparently, her Catholic mother gave birth to three illegitimate children, of which Kathleen was one. In those days it was common practice for these poor unfortunate babies to be placed in a big basket on the front of an old 'sit up and beg' bike and taken to Kilbride Chapel to have it baptised into the Catholic faith. Of course, the only concern there would be to increase the Catholic population but there was not the same consideration and importance placed on the child's well being. I have learned that her mother was housekeeping for a farmer who was a widower and he made her pregnant three times – thus the repeated trips to Kilbride Chapel with the bicycle basket! You must realise that in Ireland at this time, talking about sex was a 'no-no' and yet it was all around them. Everyone pretended that it wasn't happening and the results – the illegitimate kids – would often, eventually, be dumped in a reform school. These establishments would have been more accurately described as the first concentration camps in the world; not for adults but for unwanted children. Of course, in some cases friends or relations would take on the duty of raising these unwanted children. Kathleen was one of these lucky ones as she was fostered out to a relation who provided a caring family. When she grew up she worked in some of the local hotels around and about Brittas Bay – a great seaside resort for those who were able to have a holiday. It is at this point that, despite having being baptised into the Catholic faith, she became interested in the Church of Ireland, as it is said that she had found a bible under a pillow in one of the guest bedrooms. It is strange to think that her father belonged in fact to the Church of Ireland then she was given over to the Catholics but eventually came back to the Protestants. When you spin these wheels of fortune they can come to some canny conclusions because when you spin it to my turn it comes up where my father was a Roman Catholic. Changing her religion from Catholic to Church of Ireland would have been extremely unusual and one almighty step to take so I can only assume that my foster mother was an unusual and spirited woman at that stage in her life.

Knowing the atmosphere of antagonism between the religions it was amazing to me that Kathleen managed to change her religion. When you consider that you would be struggling to do this in this particular time and place even if you were of independent means, but when you realise that she was coming from a very basic, working class background with only the bare minimum skills it must have been so hard. When you also consider that at the time she was having a relationship with Arthur who had been mollycoddled by his grandmother and two Aunts so he wouldn't have known the meaning of independence of thought, then it becomes a phenomenal feat. She must have known that the move would result in her being ostracised. You can be assured that this would not have been a good position to be starting your married life in. Her new husband would work only intermittently so life was even more difficult than it needed to be. When you consider also that at every turn either Kathleen or Arthur took they were going to be met with scorn – ridiculed and damned by society. You do not change from one religion to another in a place like Ireland without paying a very heavy price.

Our family also included two old ladies with whom we lived from time to time in their farmhouse on the hill – Daisy and May Reynolds – who were my foster father's aunts. They worked hard and had difficult lives. Most things they did for me or for Arthur and Kathleen Donald and their family were done out of what they perceived as their duty. I didn't know then just how important those two old ladies would become in my life, nor how wonderful they were. I think I must credit them with my survival. These two women were well known locally as 'characters'. Daisy was the mouthpiece and May was the quiet orchestrater, putting Daisy's ideas and plans into action. They would beg and borrow food and other people's unwanted cast offs for me and for the rest of the family. Looking back on it now I can understand what remarkable people they were. They had 48 acres of land on a hillside. They used to let the land out to farmers for 11 months of the year (in Ireland at the time that was the maximum you could let it for), and they would get a small income paid twice a year. They would have needed all of this income plus more just to keep themselves but because my foster father didn't work regularly they were frequently forced to share what little they had with us.

We children played them up something terrible and this we can't deny, but they appeared to take it in their stride even though they were in their sixties by the time we were growing up. It must have been hard for them to cope with young children. I am now finding out for myself how tiring taking care of young children can be for an older person, now that I have my own grandchildren. Daisy and May would not have had much experience of life, as they lived in a world of their own. They were really isolated and almost became a part of folklore history in the area. Often, people in their own village wouldn't have known the Misses Reynolds personally but their oddness would have been known far and wide, as were their characters. They were the kind of people you meet only once in a lifetime. They were often the talk of households far and wide and there was always someone who would have a tale to tell about them.

As older people often do, they became victims of crime. Daisy went to the bank to collect some money after letting the land to a farmer and she was on her way home from Wicklow town when somebody put their hands on her face. As the man grabbed her bag, she screamed out. 'James, Dick, Harry!' – the names of her brothers, who were in Canada. With that the bloke had such a fright because he assumed that Daisy was able to see these people near by and he let her go and ran for his life. Daisy, not realising that her assailant had run away, climbed rapidly over the fence and crossed several fields to her cousin Dick Reynolds's farm at Sheep Hill. She kept screaming 'James Dick and Harry come quick'. This shook her up badly and Daisy would not stir out of the house for quite a while because of fear.

Daisy being Daisy overcame her fears and before long she was back into her normal stride. In those days shops stayed open until customers stopped coming in and on one occasion Daisy was in Wicklow town, doing a bit of shopping or bartering. She had seen nobody that she knew except the priest and she went up and asked him could she have a lift back. He agreed and as he dropped her off at the bottom of the cart road he said, 'Miss Reynolds, if ever you need a lift and you see my car just get in it and I will drop you off'. Of course, she took him at his word and one night she spotted his car in Wicklow and she got into the back seat. As they got to the cart road, she shouted out, 'Father, this will do me grand!' The priest nearly had a heart attack because he didn't even know that she was in the car at all. It was this sort of story that Daisy was renowned for and May would stand out too with similar tales. They were the forerunners to characters like Ena Sharples in Coronation Street in that they donned hairnets and spoke forthrightly and loudly – sometimes louder than thunder.

Daisy and May's mother, Granny Reynolds, lived till she was 95 years of age and she was truly a remarkable woman – great characters seemed to abound in the female line in the Donald family. Apart from raising her own six children she raised, as I've said, 14 children from the Titanic disaster and she also raised my foster father following the series of disasters that befell his family. I can remember her combing her long grey hair in her rocking chair and I can still see her old black bootee-type shoes that old folk used to wear in those times. Her grandfather had built the hill house for his family and she kept it going. Incidentally, he was no lazybones as he made his own headstone, his own coffin and the cart that carried the coffin to finish his life as had carried on during it.

Despite the flashy outfit that I wore when I arrived at the Donald's and Daisy and May's best efforts, I was soon in rags and living in complete poverty. It was a standard of living that is indescribable and it was certainly as low, if not lower than, any third world country standard. Shortly after I arrived and my new foster brother, Sean, had been born, my foster father lost his job and that was when the problems really started. There was no money coming in and there were now three of us children – my foster brother and my foster sister and myself. Even at this early stage the cold light of day had dawned on me.

Chapter 5

Early years with the Donalds

I started my new life with the Donald family at the Dunganstown schoolhouse. The old schoolhouse was all that was left of the town's school buildings after a fire. The schoolhouse, which had previously been the teachers' living quarters, had been salvaged by sawing the beams down at the gable end where it had been connected to the ruined school building. In its heyday, the old school house was a picturesque place – it wouldn't have been out of place on a picture postcard. There was a short driveway up from the road and a pretty little well on the left hand side. I remember that there were many trees surrounding the house including a big sycamore tree and a beech tree on the right hand side of the drive. Unfortunately, the building was well past its sell-by date and would have been somewhere in the region of 2 or 3 hundred years old when we lived there. There was a big metal weathervane in the shape of a cockerel on the roof that was totally out of proportion to the reduced size of the school-house roof. When the gales blew, the noise from this was deafening. It was always safer to move downstairs out of the way at these times because there was the ever-present fear of it coming crashing through the roof as all of the timber was so badly rotted. Wood-worms were at full gallop devouring the timbers. So, all in all, it wasn't really a safe or pleasant place to live but it was what I had to call home.

The house had big shutters that went the full length of the windows that rattled loudly when the wind blew. The walls were extremely thick and it was obviously a very cold place in the winter. One would need a trailer-load of timber to keep any heat going. There was an old ramshackle shed right outside our front door – originally used for the bicycles that had belonged to the pupils and teachers at the old school. Eventually, they built a new school where the old one had been. This was to the right of the old schoolhouse and they dug the foundations out of the hill for the building. Despite its shortcomings, I must say that it was situated in one of the most beautiful places on earth.

The beauty of Co Wicklow is something you have to experience to realise what a wonderful and lovely place it is. Even through all the hardships I endured, I was able to appreciate this beautiful place. I was able to look over the hills from where I was raised and to see for miles. From the old aunts' hill house you could actually see nine counties of Ireland. On a very clear day you could even see right across the Irish Sea to Snowdon in North Wales – it was an absolute paradise. It was indeed a very picturesque setting and I was always struck when I looked out in this direction that there was a very gentle look to the different stages of countryside that would appear. It seemed to me to have a soothing, comforting feel to the countryside (and heaven knows I needed soothing from time to time). You would be able to see over Rathdrum but when I looked out that way more often than not I would see a very dark cloud hovering over that area and we would always consider that it never seemed to stop raining in Rathdrum. If I looked a little more to my left I could see over the hills and valleys of Avoca. I'm sure some of you will know this area from watching the TV series Ballykiss-angel. I often felt a compulsion when I saw the programme myself to grab the camera and aim it at the mouth of the river. This was the centrepiece of the poem of Avoca. I find the words of the poem about the meeting of the waters are very soothing for your inner soul. I enjoyed the programme but I was surprised that they didn't tie in some of the historical features and people of the area. For example, Parnell, the great politician of his day, had lived only a matter of a mile or so away from where Ballykissangel was filmed and, of course, they never tied in the mining history of Avoca, which still leaves its scar on the beautiful countryside.

However, set against this beauty, the family I stayed with were living in extreme poverty – ugly poverty. It was a well-off community dominated by the Church of Ireland and we were one of their own. These Protestants that we lived among were proud, independent people who always maintained a 'stiff upper lip'. Whenever one went to church there was always a Christian Aid collection for the third world countries. I suppose when I look back, now that I am older, I wonder what the hell, how come these collections didn't come in my direction? Of course, I recognise the need for aid for foreign countries but what about the well-known saying 'charity begins at home'? How could anyone ignore the unbelievable poverty that people were experiencing in their own country – their own neighbourhood even – and then place money in a box to help people that they've never seen or heard of? In some cases, I suspect, these people in faraway places wouldn't even have received the money because of the corruption that prevailed. That could never have been right. It just shows you how it is impossible to explain hypocrisy.

We had some of the wealthiest families in Ireland living around us at this time and a lot of these Irish Protestant families would have been able to trace their family history back to the days of the ruling class of the British Empire. None of them appeared to be short of a penny or two and they would have had investments in many aspects of British and American businesses and in world commerce. Some of these families are still around today. There was the family of Haskins, and you've got Lord Haskins today advising the Labour Government. I remember his relations taking their part in our society – decorating the church in Dunganstown every Easter and every Christmas. They were lovely people but, like the rest of the well-to-do families of the area, they all went around with their eyes shut when it came to this one Church of Ireland family. This family was in desperate need of help but their plight was studiously ignored. It doesn't add up and to me it never will.

When I first lived in Dunganstown there used to be a lady who followed me. Don't forget that this was a rural area and not a large town or city where people would have happened to be just passing by, so it was not just a coincidence that she saw me – she had come to find me. She would always scream 'Give him back to me' and become very agitated. I particularly remember one beautiful, hot summer's day while I was going down Cullen Lane with my foster mother, this lady followed us, trailing behind us and, as usual, screaming for me to be given back to her. I was pulled into Mary Doyle's house and kept in there till the lady went away. I can still see her and her summer clothes and the fashionable, round brimmed summer hat she wore. I grew up wondering who this lady was and why she was following me and why she was screaming for me to be given back to her. There were so many questions without answers. As I got older my desire to find out exactly who this lady was got stronger. Obviously, I thought that there could be a chance that she was my real mother. Many, many years later I tracked my real mother down and she assured me that it was not her who was in my memory at that age. The mystery of who this woman was remained with me throughout my childhood and it was something that was always on my mind. It caused me many sleepless nights and nightmares. Although it was a brief period in time – probably two years or so – that she followed me, to me it was a very long period and it seemed to go on forever. I would be rocking myself to sleep at night and I would continually be remembering that lady who used to follow me.

Just in case anyone assumes that I was remembering things like this right from the day I was born, I can assure you that it took me almost a lifetime to recall this. The information I have about my very early years was all found through research. Thankfully I was successful enough in my search for my roots that I am able to back up what I found with documents and verbal accounts from people around at the time.

A nearby attraction for me in my boyhood years was Dunganstown Castle. It had, allegedly, been burnt down three times and it is believed that King James II came back to Dunganstown Castle, after the Battle of the

Boyne, and there he sat on a big stone chair and wept. When I lived in Dunganstown this chair was always referred to as a wishing chair and strangers used to stop there and make a wish but it doesn't seem to have done poor King James much good! It was in a lovely old part of the country and you could easily imagine the castle and its grounds four or five hundred years earlier. It would have been a hive of activity with its own wheat fields and hop fields all around it. They used to get all the timber for their bows and arrows from the yew trees and for general timber, they would use the woods at Dunganstown. As a young boy I used to imagine the troops coming out of the castle on horseback with bows and arrows, pikes and spears. I would re-enact the battles in my head and found it easy to picture the colours of the uniforms and the spectacular, whirling flags. I would lose myself in these imaginings for many an hour during the years I spent at Dunganstown. This part of the country was very important to the security of the eastern part of Ireland. Soldiers would have gone up to the top of the tower to check if the invaders were coming into Brittas Bay. If they spotted any intruders coming, they would use the tunnel that was situated on the hill,

71

which would lead them down to the river. They would then push the boats down into the river and be ready and waiting for the invaders to land. It was almost impossible for anyone to take them by surprise.

Dunganstown only contains a few houses dotted about and people often used to come looking for a town. However, there is no town – only a tiny settlement. In the time of King James there were probably more than a thousand people living around, and connected to, the castle and there were maybe thousands passing through the area to go to the church. There used to be a secret tunnel in the area but it had been filled in. At about the same time as those famous explorers in Egypt had found Tutankhamun's tomb in the mid-1920s, there were some workmen repairing the fence that ran along between the churchyard and the Estate. As they were digging, one of the stakes that they were driving in simply disappeared into the ground – into the secret tunnel. I don't know if they feared some sort of curse as with King Tut's tomb or had heard that the stale air could kill anyone who breathed it but the Castle owners got the workmen to fill in the tunnel straight away. No one has ever found that tunnel from that day to this. As far as I am aware it ran all the way to the river.

At one point while we were living in Dunganstown, Daisy and May decided that things weren't going to get any better unless they took matters into their own hands and gave Arthur a push. The solution they came up with was to make sure that my foster father got a job down in Tipperary in a place called Barn Park. The two old ladies were feeling the pinch financially because they were sharing what little income they had from their farm with Arthur Donald and his family. It made life impossible. My foster father got the job down in Barn Park, Co. Tipperary and we were on the move. I must have been around five at the time.

I remember the old Ford lorry that we borrowed for the move, which we loaded all our bits and pieces on and off we went to Barn Park. I can vividly recall that on the way down I was sick again and again and they got me some soda water from a little shop along the way. The Barn Park Estate was a very grand, sprawling estate and it was reputedly won and lost on the gambling tables of Monte Carlo many times. My foster father's job was as a cattle herdsman on the estate. We were there in 1947 and I remember the exceptional snow that year.

When we came out of the house, you could see mountains of snow. I don't know what it would be like for an adult but for a boy who was only about 6 or 7 years old it appeared to be one hell of a height and a terrible sight to look at. Whilst we were at Barn Park, I remember them trying to find out if they had got petrol or paraffin because in those days for the tractors they were TVO. They used to start them on petrol and then switch it over to the TVO. One time I recall them pouring this liquid onto the ground and trying to light it, though I can't recall whether it was petrol or TVO, but I'm sure that somewhere along the line they must have sorted it out. Funny the little things that stick in your mind.

We lived in a huge house on the estate. There were several large houses belonging to the estate, plus the gatehouses and then there was the main house with a very large gated entrance and an impressive driveway leading up to it. This driveway was lined with beech trees and the gateway itself had two large pillars. Sitting on top of these pillars were two stone lions. It is believed that these lions were damaged by gunfire from cannons during the Oliver Cromwell campaigns in Ireland in those far-off days.

One day when I was at Barn Park I was wandering around the estate, playing as I usually did, when I spotted an egg moving, seemingly unaided. Being a kid I was rather curious to find out how that could possibly be and as I got closer to it I could see that a rat had wrapped its tail around the egg and it was dragging it along. Most peculiar. Another memory I have of that time involved the little terrier that I had while we lived at Barn Park. At that time my foster father was keeping greyhounds. I had kept a bone back for the terrier and tried to ensure that the bone went to the terrier – not to the greyhounds that always seemed to me to be exceptionally greedy dogs. However, as I pushed the bone towards my little dog, the greyhounds made a wild dash for the bone. It was mayhem. All the dogs fought for it and one of them managed to bite my arm in the process. I looked down at my arm in panic and the blood began to pour out. As if that was not bad enough, in the blood I noticed that there were white fleshy bits and I assumed that that was my guts. This terrified me even more than the blood! My foster mother was milking cows down in the cowshed and I ran down to her and I shouted to her 'oh, my guts are running out in the blood'. All my mother did was clean it with just a rag, boiling hot water and some Jeyes fluid. There was no fuss – and certainly no sympathy or understanding. And, of course, you didn't go to the doctor's or the hospital for those sorts of things in those days.

Things weren't too bad at Barn Park for a period; my father was earning a steady living, we ate regular meals, the house was provided with the job and there was even an occasional bonus. The cattle dealers would give my foster father the odd beast for looking after the cattle. When my foster father had a mind to do something he could be as good as anybody and often better. Unfortunately he didn't have the staying power to do things right for very long. It certainly wasn't long in this case before the manager of the estate took the cattle my foster father was looking after, leaving him little to do. My foster father confronted him about it and that resulted in him getting the sack. However, my foster father went to court and lodged a case against the manager. So, there we were, back to square one, with no job and no money coming in. We were on the move again.

Life was always a struggle – mainly be-cause of my foster father's chequered work history. Sometimes though, my foster father would find temporary work or he would get a job on the forestry for a while, or he would get one of a string of jobs that he was to take on during his lifetime. He could be a hardworking man – when he was working at all – but he had this inability to hang on to work and this always caused the family problems. It was like riding a bronco at the rodeo show – it was always up and down and sometimes you would stay on for a little while but most of the time you got flung off.

After a long, difficult period out of work, my foster father finally got a job as a sexton at the Church of Ireland church in Clonmel, Co. Tipperary. This was only a part time position, making the financial situation very tight (but better than it had been when he was unemployed, of course) and meant that my father had to look after the upkeep of the Church and the school.

A couple of incidents that I remember from this time involved the cemetery that we looked out on to. Two old ladies lived next door to us and to me they were very ancient. Sadly they both died within a very short time of each other and I remember both of their coffins being carried away in a hearse. Another funeral caused great excitement because the coffin arrived with a gun belt around it. This was something outside the normal practice and therefore I didn't ever forget the sight. It turned out that it was the coffin of one the rebels who had been dug up at Mount Joy prison and it was being reburied in the cemetery. I can recall still that big leather gun belt and cartridges wrapped around the coffin and his hat and gloves placed on top. My excitement on this occasion was ignored because my foster father was not in the best of moods. This was because he was busy because of the funeral and added to that he was unable to afford the customary Woodbines that he would have smoked to mark the occasion. The price for the cigarettes – the workmen's Abdullah as they used to say – was an amount out of my father's reach. Woodbines were sold in 5's, 10's and 20's in those days and would usually have taken top priority in a working man's budget.

I also remember that on this particular day the vicar of the parish and my foster father had a disagreement. If you fell out with the vicar and you were a sexton living in their accommodation you were evicted immediately. I recall my foster father lining up a bed at the upstairs window and trying to throw it so that it landed on the vicar's head. My foster father was yet again without a job and the family was without a house.

After this, we moved to Irishtown Street in Clonmel, Co. Tipperary to live with an old chap who was very grumpy and miserable. I've lived in many houses but this was the strangest house I've ever known. I would be the first to pooh-pooh ghosts or spirits, but while I was living there, I had two experiences that I will never be able to explain. The stairs were boxed in with a little door at the bottom. This made me feel uncomfortable right from the start and I was tormented with shapes of gruesome-looking men's faces floating up the stairs and looking down at me from the ceiling. This troubled me so much that I got into a habit of rocking myself to sleep on my elbow and had this habit till I was over 13 years old.

Another disconcerting experience I had at about this time was when I was playing in the garden and suddenly looked up to the sky. I was so mystified by what I saw that I ran in to tell everyone else. I shouted out as soon as I got inside 'I saw Grandma and her rocking chair heading for the cloud!' Make of this what you like, but within one hour a telegram arrived to say that she had passed on.

While we were at the Irishtown address we had repeated floods, very bad floods at times. The water used to come right up to the door-steps of some of the houses. I remember one occasion when the floods were so bad that the pigs were washed out of their pigsties. The scene further up the river where a small crowd gathered, trying to catch the pigs as they were floating past, was a very sad affair. There were two big rivers, which met in Clonmel, and one of them was a branch that went past the gardens where I lived in the house. It was very, very nice in the summer but it wasn't very nice when it flooded.

We were there for Halloween, and I recall kids coming around knocking on everyone's doors and screaming 'I can see you through the keyhole' and running away. There would be people who took exception to this sort of carry on, and they would go out waving a hurling stick or a broom handle in a threatening manner. However by the time they got to the door the children would be gone. In those days Ireland didn't celebrate Guy Fawkes' night but they made a great celebration of Halloween. There would be groups of people out singing – 'trick or treating' – and they'd all be given tasks before they were given anything. You used to pick three-penny bits out of basins of water, apples hanging on a string and oranges in water. Adults would reward the children with cake or whatever would be at hand for their endeavour. There would be dancing and singing and piano accordions going and people all dressed up. It was a very exciting period for youngsters and the adults also enjoyed these festivities; but to me it was new because I was coming into the age of noticing these things. I would have been about seven or eight years old.

It was these better memories that I would try to concentrate on while rocking myself to sleep on an empty stomach, cold and demented by nasty images floating all around me. While I recall the ghostly experiences I am aware that they might sound strange. If somebody else had told me of these happenings and ghostly tales I would think that they were having me on. I can assure you that they did happen. I don't know if the house was haunted or not but whilst we were there, there were certainly some strange things happening.

As a child living in a country area you have the year very clearly divided. You have Christmas time when the church has to be decorated for the Christmas Day service, for example. This is when we would fetch out the templates that fitted the windows. These were wooden frames covered by mesh where we would stick the ivy, holly and the moss background. In this way every window would be done out like a picture off a postcard. The big font by the main doors of the church would be 'camouflaged'. It was so well done that you would think it was the remains of a trunk of a tree, which had been totally taken over with the moss and ivy. There was no doubt that little Miss Haskins who was in charge of these preparations was a true professional in her art. No part of the church was left out of these frantic preparations for Christmas day – the pulpit and the big eagle for the prayer book would be elaborately decorated and in the porch they would create a crib for baby Jesus with angels, donkeys and all the trimmings that would go with the period. We had blooms even in the dead of winter – there would be every type of flower on display from people's greenhouses. One area of the church that I particularly remember at this time was the old roll of honour for those who lost their lives in the First and Second World Wars. All of the ex-military people would always place their hand on the scroll when passing and would have their little quiet minute in silence and remembrance.

Incidentally, it seems strange that the great many Irish people who lost their lives in the two world wars were only commemorated in this type of memorial in the Church of Ireland. There was no formal commemoration outside the churches for them of the contribution they made towards peace in Europe. I suppose that for this reason a lot of people don't realise the Irish sacrifice. A great deal more Roman Catholics than Protestants lost their lives and it is a great scandal that these people shouldn't be given proper respect. But if you go to Glencrea in County Wicklow you will find a very special memorial to commemorate the dead of two German planes that crashed in the Wicklow mountains. This memorial spot is a very special, peaceful place but where else would you find a country that would honour in such a lavish way the German dead but give no consideration whatsoever for their own fellow citizens?

Back to my memories of Dunganstown church. It was a lovely old Norman church and of course in my day it was completely shrouded in ivy. I remember that there was a hole in the ivy where the great huge key for the door was kept – today you wouldn't be able to leave the key lying about. The church was in a wonderful setting with a wood to the south end, the castle on its eastern side and all around were the big trees that bordered the farmland around the castle (where every jackdaw would seem to come and squeal out a chorus as the evenings closed in). There was the river that trundled its way from Rathnew and then swung around the castle wood, making its way to join up with the ocean.

The church was also lavishly decorated for Easter and for Harvest time when the church would be ablaze with colour and the aromas of all the wonderful flowers, fruit and vegetables made it seem like heaven to me. I would have to fetch all the moss, ivy and all of the different varieties of laurel leaves, yew tree branches and so on then I would leave the women – the experts – to arranging the splendid displays. There would be apples, grapes, pears, oranges, all of the different ranges of nuts, turnips, carrots, parsnips, sheaves of wheat and oats. I hope nobody is listening, but I have to say that I tried out every edible piece of fruit and vegetable. I can personally vouch for the fact that this locally grown produce could not be beaten for taste and quality.

Many people have commented since that they are surprised that I could appreciate such beauty – and retain these impressions throughout my life – amid such poverty and deprivation, but I would find it truly unbelievable to be able to ignore such beauty no matter what your circumstances.

Chapter 6

First Escape

During the period after we left Barn Park, my father's court case regarding the stolen cattle was always a topical subject and one that kept coming up and then going away. As the court date got closer we thought we were going to 'be in the money' as the saying goes. It would've been a lot of money in those days and certainly to us. However, in reality, it wasn't a great deal – it would have only been a couple of hundred quid once everything was settled. What we were going to do with this money was nobody's business. We planned over and over again how we would spend it and how we would have a different life. The one plan that we always came back to though, involved emigration; a complete escape from the hard life that we were all suffering. My foster-father had made up his mind that he wanted to go to Australia.

But he was a contrary character. If Arthur Donald were in Australia he would want to be back in Dunganstown and vice versa. Sure enough, the court case came around and he got his settlement from the court case. It was all hands to the pump to get ready to head for Australia. We packed up what we could carry and then dug a big hole and buried a lot of the stuff we weren't taking. All the rest of our possessions we simply dumped in the river. We children worried about what would happen to the few bits of toys that we had between us. We came up with the idea that if we dug a deep enough hole then the toys would all end up in Australia by the time we got there. So we buried all of these toys, pieces of old teddies and prams and what have you. It's strange but we really believed, that's my foster sister and myself, that we would end up seeing them all again in Australia. The toys that couldn't be buried had to go in the very large river at the bottom of the gardens. We got our tickets and headed for England first. I don't know whether this was Arthur's way of not really 'biting the bullet' by taking a small step before he took the bigger, more final step of going to Australia.

We ended up going on a cattle boat that was headed for England. Its destination was Birkenhead but we were headed for Manchester. The ship was very old and decrepit. I can remember that there were holes in the table for fitting mugs into. In those days there were no plastic cups as we have today and you would put your mug in one of the holes in the big table so that you didn't lose it when the ship pitched and rolled. There was a big herd of cattle in the hold underneath us so the smell must have been almost unbearable but to us children it was exciting because it was something new and different. Because of the money my foster father had received for his court case, we were able to buy meals as and when we needed them. This availability of food was a big change for our constitution – and a very welcome one. To be able to eat what and when we wanted was sheer luxury. When we arrived in Birkenhead on Merseyside, we had to get organised for our onward journey and the only choice of travel for us was the train to Manchester.

My memories of Manchester will stay with me until the day I die. When we arrived in Manchester all we saw was rubble and debris from all the bombs that were dropped during the war. Though we didn't realise it immediately this was to affect our stay. There was very little accommodation in the city centre due to the war but there was a huge amount of work available for builders and labourers.

The scenes of desolation were all around us but I do remember, among this desert of rubble and debris, there was a beautiful park with flowers blooming. Manchester seems to be ignored by many people when thinking of World War Two and they don't take on board the number of bombs that were dropped on this highly populated northern city. From what I've been told, many, many people were killed during that time. Most people would think that it was just London and Coventry that took the hammerings but I can assure you that those people in Manchester would have a different tale to tell.

We children were being dragged around, walking the streets trying to find somewhere to stay. In the end we couldn't get anywhere except a women's hostel and we all ended up being put up with old ladies in a big old building. It seemed to be one of only a few that had escaped the bombing. My foster father was not allowed to stay with us, of course, as it was for women only, though they made an exception for us kids under the circumstances. Arthur had to sleep in the park on one of the benches at night so it was a good job it was the height of summer. As hot it as it was, it wasn't a very easy time for my foster mother, I'm sure, knowing that her husband was sleeping in the park and us children were with her in this old people's home where there were some very odd characters, to say the least. Some of the old ladies would be sleep walking and wouldn't know what day of the week it was and for children to be amongst that lot was certainly not the best start for us in a new country. We must have been a bit bewildered and it must have been a very difficult experience for my foster mother to have to cope with three children, one of them a very young child. We had to tramp the streets day in and day out while getting nowhere – it was very depressing. I remember one of the old ladies gave me a Mickey Mouse that was made of lead. Its odd isn't it, but I thought the world of that Mickey Mouse. I would carry him everywhere and lose him and find him, but I lost him once too many times and could not find him anywhere but I still remember him very well to this day.

My foster father had a heart of gold for sure but he had very little sense. He would often go to areas in Manchester that had been bombed out and he'd find a group of lads and give them handfuls of change. You see, though the Irish pound was accepted in shops, the Irish coins were not. To him, they were useless and it was pointless to carry them. Of course, the money would not last for long spending it in this fashion. There was certainly going to come a day when he would have been very glad of all that loose change. I was unable to see the sense in what he was doing and feared that he would regret it later, although we were soon distracted by other things during that difficult time.

Manchester displayed the horrors of World War Two not just in the destruction of the buildings but in the people as well. Everywhere we went there were people who had received injuries from this war. There were people with legs missing, as well as arms, noses, ears. The whole thing was a horrific scene for a child to take on board, particularly when you hadn't seen anything like it before. We saw all the different soldiers and sailors' uniforms and of course there were servicemen from all over the world, coming and going.

While we were in Manchester we felt we had to visit Piccadilly. We wouldn't have felt that we had really been to Manchester unless we had been to Piccadilly. Most people would think of Piccadilly in London but of course there's a Piccadilly in Manchester too and that was certainly the place to head to if anyone were to visit Manchester in those days and we found it well worth a visit. Meanwhile, the daily search for a house just went on and on, but with no success. We as children didn't realise the full extent of what was going on but I'm sure, looking back now, that for my foster mother in particular it must have been a very difficult time. She must have been at her wit's end – seeing everything going towards such a sad end. They had waited so long for that small amount of compensation money from the court case only to see it all go to waste along with all their dreams.

This situation must have been very, very haunting for my foster parents. After almost a month of being in Manchester, the cold light of day appeared to be dawning and they realised that there was no way out of this mess. Now, for my father there must have seemed no choice but to head back to Dunganstown as quickly as possible, whilst he still had the fare to pay for it. So after a month's stay in Manchester we made the reverse journey all the way back to Co. Wicklow, Ireland. It seemed an even longer journey on the way back than it had when we were on the way to Manchester, looking forward to an exciting new life. It had turned out that with us three children in tow, my foster mother and father had very few prospects in Manchester. However, I can assure you that the prospects in Dunganstown, Co. Wicklow in 1949 had even less to offer us and that's saying something. Nonetheless Dunganstown was what it was going to be. Now, with hindsight, I would have thought it would have been better for him, when he had taken the plunge by going Manchester, to have gone outside the city centre. There, perhaps he could have found a place to live and then work in Manchester where there was loads of work in particular building occupations.

After the long, depressing trip back, we landed in Wicklow with just a couple of suitcases and a few bob in loose change (the few coins that had escaped Arthur's bouts of generosity with the local children) to our names. My foster father approached a taxi driver who he knew. He told the taxi driver that Aunt Daisy would pay his fare when we got back. However, the taxi driver was familiar with the Reynolds' house in Dunganstown and knew that neither Aunt Daisy nor Aunt May would have had a penny to bless themselves with, never mind pay for their nephew's taxi fare. The taxi driver, despite knowing this, kindly said, 'as it is for Miss Reynolds I'll do it'. He dropped us off at the bottom of the cart road leading up to the old hill house. This was three fields off the road, up a very rough cart road so we trudged the rest of the way. I'm sure it must have been a horrendous sight for May and Daisy when they looked out and saw my foster father and mother and us three children struggling up the pathway. They probably knew straight away that Arthur was out of work, would have spent all of his money and the only thing he would have is bits and pieces in a couple of suitcases. We, as children, could not fully appreciate that it would have been quite shattering for them to have to take us in again because they themselves would have had an everyday struggle just to stay alive. They would by this time have been very weary of having to prop him up as they had done throughout his life. Daisy was never shy and she asked very straightforwardly 'Arthur what are you going to do now?' before he had even got his hat off. Arthur though, knew how to deal with Daisy and May, as he had had many years of practice. He just replied 'put the kettle on, and let's have a cup of tea' and poor old May was in the background, nervously rubbing her face with the palms of her hands as she climbed into the huge fireplace to get the kettle going.

The hill house didn't have any of the modern amenities such as running water so we had to fetch the water at all times of the year. This meant us walking for a good half a mile in the summer time, as the old well nearer the house would dry up. The fuel they used for the fire was wood because they didn't have money to buy coal or turf. For firewood they relied on bushes that they got from the hill or old bits of trees that had been blown down. The open fireplace in the hill house was huge – it had a car axle across it to hang the hooks for pans. You could nearly burn the trunk of a tree in one go, so you could imagine the problem of keeping it supplied with firewood. To keep a kettle going, to boil water, to cook, bake, or wash always meant having to go and fetch firewood. Of course, that was my first job on our return. It seemed that nothing had changed.

When we had the chance to look around us at the hill house we found Daisy and May were in dire straits. They were now getting on in years and the tremendous snowstorms of 1947 had resulted in their being isolated in the farmhouse for several weeks. Things had got so bad and they had suffered from the cold so much that they had to resort to removing and chopping up the floorboards in the back bedroom to use as fuel. This, of course, had ruined their house but they had no alternative if they were to survive. To this day I still puzzle about why the local community, knowing that two old spinsters plus their 95-year old mother, Granny Reynolds, were alone and stranded in the farmhouse, did not make some attempt to help them all. Many of the locals were farmers with tractors or horses and they could surely have made their way up to the hill house to dig the way out for the three old ladies and perhaps bring them some food and fuel. It's just one more mystery for me to ponder in my old age. Surveying the disaster area that was Daisy and May's home and was to be our home again for a while did not make us any happier to be back in Ireland.

Chapter 7

Daily Life

By the time we came back from England I was old enough to work regularly to make a contribution to the family although I was still, of course, attending school – most of the time!

I went to the Dunganstown School but it was, in effect, only a holding place for the local children, as most ended up going to colleges or boarding school. There were only about eighteen pupils ranging from six years old to fourteen – mixed, boys and girls. Virtually all of the children went on from Dunganstown School to further education with a large percentage of them going onto private boarding schools. These children came from wealthy farming families within the Church of Ireland community. I would have said they were not short of a bob or two and so the school was often used as place to send them until they reached a standard of education, or the age, to go further. Very few children would stay on at Dunganstown beyond about twelve years old but for me things were different. I left that school at the age of thirteen and was unable to read or write. One of the reasons for that was that the teacher we had was not qualified. It was just a bit of a made up job for the teacher, no question about standards were asked as it was presumed that we would get the appropriate teaching when we moved on. Even Sean, my foster brother, went on to the Christian Brothers' School in Wicklow and gained this learning. I don't think that this was ever even considered for me. Sean was considered to be the bright one and the one that would benefit most from further education. I was treated like an idiot who was capable of working hard and doing simple jobs, so I was not in need of an education. That would have been bad enough but I was also treated worse than the others. When I had to light the fire in the school I would have to move back and sit at the back so all of the well fed and well clothed children would sit nearest to the fire. Though I was the one who had lit the fire and I was the one who was hungry and in rags, it was me who had to sit at the back and get the least heat. It certainly made me become very rebellious in my mind and take a very dim view of this treatment. I suppose the teacher wasn't equipped to deal with such a disturbed person, particularly as she wasn't even qualified to teach. No one in the school would have had the experience in dealing with this kind of situation because all the children there were normally from stable homes and pretty well off families – if not extremely rich families.

Although this lack of education certainly didn't help, I'm sure that I would have had severe problems in life anyway as a result of my experiences during my early years. I was continually made aware of the fact that I was not a real member of the family. It would be a commonplace that when people asked Daisy or May, 'Oh, who are these children?' the reply would be along the lines of 'these are the Donald children' and when they further inquired 'Who is this little lad?' the reply would be 'That's the lad they adopted'. It was always up in my face. I have got no doubt that any child having to face that kind of insecurity, rejection and isolation is going to be badly affected.

Also, my foster sister and brother were always better dressed than me. I suppose the people that Daisy would get the second-hand clothes from would think that although we were all a bit of a problem, the two natural Donald children were more local than I was. I was the one who was adopted and brought into the area and that should not have happened in their opinion – that's the only explanation I can think of. I was given only old bits of rags to wear. I was always in desperate need of new clothes and yearned to be looked after in a civilized manner. To me it appeared that people in the area, and in the family, seemed to take the view that I didn't have the right to these things. The clothes that I wore were falling apart; generally speaking I wore all my clothes until they literally fell to pieces. Daisy would try to find me someone else's hand-me down clothes to replace my dirty old rags. Of course, in these circumstances, washing or anything like that was almost non-existent. You might get a shirt washed now and again but more often than not it didn't happen. There was no such thing as a washing machine; it was boiling water and soap. Clothes were washed in a bucket or a bowl and that would be your wash. For anyone who hasn't had this experience you can't possibly comprehend the whole situation, for example I would see pictures of toothbrushes and toothpaste in old discarded magazines and I would think, 'Oh God, these people must be very rich to be able to afford all this fancy stuff'. Although people take toothbrushes and toothpaste for granted, I had never even seen them until I came to England. That will give you some idea of the standards to which I was accustomed.

It wasn't just me, however, who endured most of this deprivation but the family I lived with too. None of them would have had toothbrushes or toothpaste or any other luxuries; things like that just weren't a priority. This being the case it was a lot easier for me to spend my time in the hills or on my own or with the animals rather than with people who judged me. I felt that there was such a gap between my self and ordinary people. This gap was so wide and unreachable it was easier for me to make a life on my own. I would rather communicate with animals and with nature in the raw state than to be trying to communicate with people who would disregard me just because of what I wore and how I smelled. I would often be in school dressed in rags and everyone would keep clear of me. The atmosphere and the environment for a person of my age was quite unbelievable and sometimes unbearable.

When you think back on it you wonder how a person could survive with that being his lot. Oddly enough it never really got me down; I was quite happy with being on the hills with the goats and the rabbits and everything else that the hills had to offer. I was happy enough on my own because I never had the ambition to belong to the society I witnessed outside my own little world. Even when I had to play a part in the real world, I would be fetching wood for the fires, looking after cattle, thinning turnips or mangling beetroot to try and get a few bob to put food on the table. Being with other people was never pleasant or relaxing for me.

It's only in later years that I look back and think 'Did that really happen?' You have to pinch yourself to realise that you have gone through a nightmare and nothing could have been done about it. I was just a victim of rejection, snobbery, and discrimination. When I think about my life in those days, I would be out thinning and mangling the beetroot and turnips from early morning till late at night in the springtime and the money that I would earn would never be mine. It would have to be handed in to buy food. Some of the people that I did odd jobs for would give me eggs as they didn't always have money. Sometimes they would even give me a hen as I loved hens and still do. I was once given a Chinese Bantam hen. They are just heavenly, with silky feathers all the way down to their feet. The one I had was so friendly and it was so tame that Daisy just couldn't get over how I treated it. I would be talking to it as if it was a human being and she would shake her head and say 'that poor eejit out there thinks he's talking to someone, God love him'.

As I grew up I was, in effect, used as a slave to gather the wood for the fire and it was an arduous, ongoing task. It was like painting the Forth Bridge in that by the time you got to the end you were starting again. I would often go up on the hills to collect the wood and would have to walk miles to get it. Sometimes the load of wood would be so heavy and awkward that I would get tired and need to lie down. I would lie in the rough grass and often think about the lady who had followed me when I was just a toddler. Who was this lady? What was she to do with me? Why did she want me? That would always haunt me. You could say I was desperate to find out who that person was and as I got older I often wondered, could it have been my real mother? If I was to meet her, my own real mother, what an experience, what a great, great day that would be, I imagined. At least then I could say I really have a mother. I would imagine that I had just met her, got to know her and touched her and talked to her. It would have been like winning the lottery to me in those far off days but that wasn't to be just then. It wasn't until many years later that I was to come face-to-face with the woman who had given birth to me.

For me as boy, the hills were mainly a sanctuary – a place where I could be alone with my own thoughts. It was like being in a very spiritual place as it was so peaceful. Your thoughts could go on forever and you weren't concerned whether people were giggling at the state of your clothes, what you had or what you didn't have. I just made friends of the wild goats, rabbits, hares, foxes and all of the birds. The pheasants would fly up beside me and frighten the life out of me as they disturbed the total silence. In the summer you could hear the corncrakes and the grass-hoppers and you could drown in the cobwebs that clung to the branches and the bushes. It was like a painting, with the yellow gorse bushes and the purple and white heather all blending in together with the brown grass. With these wonderful colours and the beautiful setting, it was as if God had painted the picture himself.

The silence would often be broken with Daisy's shouting 'Where are you Derry, where are you Derry?' They never called me Derek, always Derry. As I got nearer, she would shout 'Glory be to God, we've been waiting for a cup of tea and you out with your animals I suppose'. Then she would clock me one for being around all these animals and keeping her waiting for the firewood, as I would often doze off in the heather. Daisy used to warn me 'One of these days you'll have them leeches shimmy into your mouth when you are asleep up in the heather'. This worried me desperately and I would check my arms and legs because I thought these creatures would end up having little ones and they'd be in my veins. Whenever I used to have a sleep in the heather, I would wake up wondering if I had had the pleasure of any of these things jumping down my throat. There'd be huge big beetles crawling all over me when I got up, but these creatures never bothered me. I could listen continually to the birds singing, I envied these birds. I envied their freedom and I envied that they were doing as they wanted. They provided me with a great sort of therapy in one way or another though.

Apart from having to work at gathering firewood, I had ways of earning money, as did all lads during that time. Some of the lads would come from the town to lamp rabbits on people's farms. Daisy knew some of the lads and they would come out and lamp rabbits on her farm. To me this was such an exciting business – to think that they were going out with the dogs and lamps, hunting for rabbits in the middle of the night. I longed and yearned for the day when I would be allowed to go out with these people to take part in this very exciting event. One day these lads came around and I asked them could I go out with them? Up until that point nobody wanted to be bothered with a young lad following them around in the middle of the night while hunting. I suppose they were frightened that we would end up breaking a leg or something and they'd have to go and explain to people what had happened. When they allowed to me to go with them I remember feeling so elated that it was like winning a ticket to see Kilkenny in the Wexford plain in the All Ireland at Croke Park for the next hundred years!

I was so excited and I watched as they gathered their gear for the hunt. They used a huge battery attached to a torch, and they'd have a dog. They would shine the light on the rabbit and the dog would immediately head for the rabbit. In the light the poor rabbit would be totally dazzled and an easy target. Then the boys picked the rabbits up and tied them by their legs onto what looked like broom handles. They would put a pair of rabbits together. When they returned from a hunt they sometimes would have 50 to 100 rabbits carried between them on these big poles. I will never forget the excitement that I felt during these nights under the moon and the stars with total peace in the countryside. When we returned with all these rabbits you would think that we had won the lottery we were that pleased with ourselves.

These hunts were dead easy in the summer. We often used a blackthorn stick with a big knob on the end of it. We would go in to the hills and find rabbits fast asleep in a 'seat' as we used to call them and we used to clonk them on the top of the head with this stick. The poor rabbit would not have known what hit it. We would bring them back to be either sold or to go into the pot. Others would use snares or netting; often people from Dublin used to come down and they sometimes used nets. They'd block up the holes and send a ferret in and all the rabbits would bolt into these nets over the holes. They would also have nets further out in the fields to catch the ones that found another way out that the lads hadn't thought about. You just can't imagine the kind of excitement that it gave a young lad like me – and yet it cost nothing. It cost nobody a penny. It was just sheer joy to be involved in this sort of thing.

Other people went out ferreting. They would have a ferret with a bell on its neck and when the ferret found its prey it would shake it around, obviously making its kill. The men would be listening to the ground to find out where this would be going on and they would go deep down and explore the hole to see if they were in the right area. They would dig down and almost every time they would be right on top of where the kill had just taken place. It was amazing how many rabbits they would get through this method – dozens in one go. Others also used rabbit traps but to me that was a very brutal way of doing it. I would often go to these traps the following day to check what had been caught and time and again there was just a leg there or I'd find a poor rabbit being held by the last bit of tissue on its leg. If it were a very frosty, snowy, cold period the poor rabbit could have been in that trap all night and be frozen solid. It was these experiences that made me consider traps to be one of the most brutal and cruel ways of catching a rabbit. Snaring could be almost as cruel. A lot of people would forget where they set the snares. Sometimes they could be setting the snares in fields where there are thousands of acres and it wasn't difficult to forget where you set them. This would prove to be a problem as some of the rabbits would end up being starved, choked or taken by foxes. It was certainly a very cruel business and it's odd how you could teach country children to do these cruel things and never realise that they were cruel practices. It's only when you get older and you're able to think for yourself that you can see the grotesque cruelty that was involved.

Myxomatosis was to have a devastating effect on the rabbit population in the area. It was the most inhuman, unchristian act that could ever have been dreamt up. I remember the rabbits with their swollen heads and their eyes all runny with white pus. If they heard a bit of noise, they went to where the noise was because they couldn't see at all.

There were millions of rabbits left in this state. It affected a lot of people as well because many depended upon the poor old rabbit for their survival – either to eat or to swap for a piece of bread or something. I can appreciate that the rabbits were causing enormous problems for farmers in Ireland during that time but there could surely have been other ways to deal with them that didn't involve such brutality and such an uncivilized way of dealing with it. I remember around our school at the height of the Myxomatosis outbreak there were dozens of these rabbits all huddled up waiting to die in their horrible state.

Apart from rabbitting, I did many other jobs. As a child I would help out at Charlie Heavener's farm. Many times Charlie would want to pay me for the work but never actually get around to it though his wife was very good to us so I never really minded. Instead his wife would pay me in other ways. She once gave me a turkey hen and that turkey laid thirteen eggs. So when they had hatched I had those thirteen turkeys plus the mother. At the time when I had these turkeys we were living back in the schoolhouse. The house was a two up and two down. Believe it or not, I kept my turkeys in the house and when you think that there were fourteen turkeys next door to the kitchen, you can imagine the smell! It certainly caused a few rows between the church wardens and my foster father, although he wasn't particularly bothered about it. These turkeys grew and at Christmas time a van would come to collect the turkeys from the farmers in the area, to supply the Christmas trade. The van driver had a shop called Fleming's in Barndarrig. My foster father sold my fourteen turkeys to him at Christmas time. I had assumed that when the turkeys were sold that I would get a long pair of trousers at least, but that didn't happen. The same people would collect the blackberries that I had picked in the autumn. It was a very prickly job and I would be torn to pieces trying to get through the bushes so with the blue juice of the blackberries all over you and your own red blood mixed amongst it you would look a good old state. We used to use that very common utensil for this type of work in the poorer end of the market – the well and truly trusted old sweet tin. It was the tin can that shopkeepers would store the bonbons and toffees in. In the unending quest for food I would do various other jobs. For example, if there were areas in the field that weren't harvested, I would go along and scythe it down myself and get the crop in. I would follow potato pickers and pick up all the spuds that were left behind after the picker had finished there. I would save all these leftovers for my turkeys.

Quite frequently the work that I had to do was organised for me by my foster father. On one occasion he had heard about a bit of casual work going at a house renovation in Kilcandra. Of course, this was short-term work but that was the sort of work that he liked best, unfortunately. It happened that at the same time I could have started work for a farmer who had a very large garden business as well as a substantial farm. This would have been a long-term job for me with a view to training me in the business. But Arthur Donald was having none of this and insisted that I had to start the job with him in Kilcandra. The work, which would be over in a couple of months, was doing up a house for people who lived in South Africa and who would only use this house every two or three years for a holiday. I had to cycle eight miles to this job on a clapped-out push bike and most of the roads were like climbing huge mountains so you can imagine that I was not pleased about having to take this job in preference to the other one.

Another job that Arthur put me forward

for was fetching a horse from Jim O'Brien's farm and taking it over to the forge at Barndarrig. James O'Brien's son didn't take the horse nor did my foster father take him, and that was because my foster father was very good at volunteering me to do jobs for other people – he took a great deal of pride out of it.

When I got to the farm, my foster father was already talking to Jim O'Brien and Mrs O'Brien made me a cup of tea. She couldn't believe I was wearing the trousers that I had on, because they were so small. She said to my foster father, 'Can't you get the child a better pair of trousers than that? They are no good to him in the middle of winter, he must be frozen.' Of course my legs were red and blue with the cold and I was wearing them because the old pair I had fell apart. Daisy had got two pairs of trousers for Sean but normally when she got Sean a pair of trousers they were of better quality than the trousers I received. The trousers I got were meant to fit people three or four years younger than I was. To be honest they were just like briefs on me. Mrs O'Brien couldn't believe they would have a lad of my age running around in that state.

Trousers or no trousers, I had to take this

horse over to the forge at Barndarrig and to have new shoes put on him and it was a hell of a day. It was pouring with rain with a very, very high wind and it was extremely cold as it was in December. When I got over to the forge, old Jack Burke asked if I would like a cup of tea and, of course, when you are cold and wet, a cup of tea goes down very well. So Jack got out the teapot and poured more water into it and put a handful of tea in and he got his bellows out and started fanning up the fire. He poured this tea into an old mug and he asked me if I'd like some sugar. I said I did and he fixed that for me. 'Here you are lad, that'll warm you up well'. He went about his business, shoeing the horse I'd brought down. I tasted this tea and I couldn't believe it! I thought Daisy and May's tea was bad, but this tea was horrendous, the spoon stood up in it, it was so strong. The first chance I got, even though I was desperate for a warm drink, when he was occupied in some other area I just dumped the tea. But I still remembered to say thank you very much.

Work didn't always go to plan. One year I had just finished doing a lot of thinning and potato picking and stone picking for various farmers when I met Dick Reynolds who had heard that I wasn't bad at the work I did. He asked me if I would pull some very long weeds out of his beet, mangle and turnips and he would pay me at the end of the week. It was a daunting job as the weeds were twice as tall as I was and in the dew I was drenched by just touching them. I pulled these weeds as he requested and at the end of the week I went up to see Dick Reynolds at Sheep Hill about the pay he had promised me. Well, he started shouting at me that I had done nothing and was good for nothing. I ran as fast as my legs would carry me out of his big long driveway. Several weeks later he was driving by the old school house in Dunganstown and had stopped to talk to my foster father, he shouted to me as to why I hadn't come back to finish the weeding for him. 'Well,' I replied, with my head held high, 'you told me that you wasn't paying me and that's the reason why I didn't go back.' He sat in his car and started to laugh loudly and my foster father joined in with him thinking that all this was very funny. I failed to see the funny side of it because I had to been put down all my young life. Seeing the scowl on my face, Arthur Donald started shouting at me saying, 'You knew Goddamn well that the man would pay you, he was only having a crack with you!' Well, I didn't think much to his crack.

Several months after this I was working for Mrs Flint doing her garden and somebody passed by and asked 'Have you heard the news? Dick Reynolds of Sheep Hill has been killed in a motor accident.' Of course it was a big shock to hear this news. Mrs Flint was so upset by it that she forgot to pay me for the work I'd done in her garden. Some reckoned that a fault with his car had caused the accident but others speculated that it was a goat that he was trying to avoid. Some people said that it was a heart attack. But whatever the reason, the result was tragic and I felt particularly sad because we had left on such a bad note. I never had the chance to understand him better nor to understand his joke. I never personally received any money for the job I did but for all I know he may have paid my foster father. If so, the money would have ended up in the Beehive pub.

Food was always a problem. The staple diet would be potatoes – the good old Irish spud. These wouldn't be just a side dish as they are today; they would often be the only food we would eat all day. Mostly we ate what was available from the countryside – things such as apples and blackberries – and we often started the day with porridge flavoured with salt and made with goat's milk or water according to what was available. Another delicacy was something we called 'goody', which was bread dunked in hot sweet tea. We rarely had what you might call a 'proper meal'. Despite being surrounded by animals – my turkeys, birds, goats and so on – we would not often kill one of these to put on our own table as they were desperately needed to sell for money. The occasional exception to this would be the odd rabbit killed for the pot. What a day that would be – especially if May had been able to bake a few cakes as well!

When May had a bit of money or some flour she would bake. We would always be able to tell how the money situation was by what she was baking. Sometimes she would bake plain cakes and sometimes they would have raisins and sometimes, if we were really lucky, we would get rock cakes. Some of the bread Daisy and May baked was something we had named tramlines. We called it tramlines because it shaped into lines of dough as it cooked on the firewood.

Clothes were another source of worry for me on a daily basis. They were a constant embarrassment to me because I looked such a disgrace. My trousers would always have holes and, as I've already said, were usually too small. Even when I got hold of some second hand clothes – and I know that Daisy tried very hard to find them for me – they were not good quality or really suitable for the life I led and they soon became full of holes. When you think of the nature of the things I was doing, the wear and tear on my clothes was horrendous. We didn't go to many places without coming across barbed wire, thorns and bits of branches. Climbing into hedges to get blackberries and crab apples always proved disastrous for clothes. Footwear was also a real problem. The rough ground in the fields would rip the life out of even very strong boots, never mind the type of Wellies I would wear trekking through the hills. Wellies were often the only type of footwear I had but they were completely and utterly useless for this type of life. I would often be in the hills, running after goats, and one of my Wellies would get caught in an old bush and it would virtually slice the whole sole off one side of my boot. It wouldn't be long before I had the water coming in and I would be paddling in the slop inside my boot. So, I arrived home with rather wet feet on a regular basis. What made it worse was that I often didn't have any socks on. This would result in the Wellies chafing my legs and as the area became too sore I would often roll the boots down to avoid the rubbing. Of course, being in short trousers didn't help matters either. During the winter I used to wrap my feet in rags to act as socks but despite my efforts I still used to get tremendous chilblains and the pain from those would keep me awake at night. They reckoned a cure for it was to wee in a bucket and stick your feet in it to help heal the chilblains, though I tried that and the pain was something you would never forget. Sometimes the chilblains got infected and my feet would be a mass of pus. So, in winter I was in a real mess and often in great pain.

Amidst all of this pain, especially at night, I would often recall the lady who used to follow me all around when I was four years old. This would always come back to haunt me, as I would want to know who this woman was. I wanted to know why she wanted me to be given to her. I had no idea who this person could be but as I got older I assumed that it was my mother and therefore my interest became stronger and stronger. I longed to solve this mystery.

Whenever I broached this subject with Daisy or May, they would just go silent and they would shrug me off by suggesting that I had imagined it or that I was being stupid. They would ask me why did I keep thinking of something that didn't exist and wouldn't I be better going and getting some wood for the fire? That was how they dealt with it. Though they were very keen on telling me that I was adopted and fostered, nobody would tell me anything as to why or how I became adopted. They would never tell me anything to do with my family, or where I was before I came to live with the Donalds, or where I came from and therefore I was left in a land of confusion and with more questions than answers. My questions were so important to me but they never could compete with the question of the day to day survival of the family.

It didn't matter if we were living at old Daisy's in the loft or down at the old school-house, we never had electricity, we didn't have gas, we didn't have coal nor turf. The only fuel we had to burn was the firewood that we would collect in the hedges or on the hills and if we didn't collect it we didn't have a fire. We didn't have a radio or a television and while many poor people in Ireland had radios, for us even this was a luxury too far. This might give you an idea of the extreme poverty I experienced during my upbringing.

Life wasn't all bad however, as I grew older I found a way of catching the goats on the hill above Daisy's and I would take them home and after a great deal of effort would at least have some goats milk. I ended up with quite a number of these goats as they would have kids and they would often attract other goats, which meant that at least we had a chance of getting a spot of milk. Probably the goats' milk was our salvation because it would have been the only bit of proper nourishment that we would have had. The young goats were heavenly, they were wonderful little things and I loved them dearly and looked after them with the best care I possibly could give them. I would almost treat them just as humans. I also made them part of my life, part of the games I played all the time. I imagined that I was a rancher and the goats were my horses or cattle and on other days they were simply my friends. I have been drawn to animals all my life and find it unbelievable how anybody could mistreat an animal. When I hear about people being cruel to animals it breaks my heart because animals can be the finest friends anyone could have and nobody has a right to be cruel to them.

These goats that I started raising and having milk from, caused a lot of complaining from the people who used Daisy's land to either till to grow crops or for grazing their animals. The goats would roam around. When the tenant farmers had done the tillage or when the corn was coming up, the goats would graze on the new shoots of the corn, much to the annoyance of those using the land. I would have to have my goats penned in and move them around from different places so that they could have something to eat. This meant springtime for me would be very hard work indeed and I was often in trouble over them. Daisy and May would play hell into me because of the goats grazing on the new corn. But they were always saying to me 'isn't it time you milked the goats, because we need some milk?' so it appeared that so long as they got the milk they were happy and would turn a blind eye to the problems the goats caused. As far as I was concerned they wanted miracles but nevertheless I had to try and perform them.

I loved the goats that I called mine on the hillside but disaster was to befall them. It was a great, great shock and caused a lot of sadness when the Forestry Department cleared the goats from the hills and planted trees. What a great loss to the whole of the community this was. The goats were shot so that the trees could grow and they even buried a mesh into the ground so that the rabbits couldn't burrow underneath. It's strange to return to that spot now to see those trees. They are now 40 to 50 feet high. They were not even saplings on the hills when I wandered there with my friends the goats.

A further day-to-day problem in the family's life was Arthur's moods. On his return from the pubs, my adopted dad would regularly beat me with his belt and sometimes would lift me right off the ground with a kick, which often caused me to land underneath the table in the room. When he was 'in drink', Arthur was frequently awkward, unpredictable and violent and would often take it out on me and the other children but the one who bore the brunt of his drunken moods was my foster mother. She tried desperately to keep the peace and to ensure that nothing happened, or was said, to upset her husband. This was a thankless task, however, and did not improve her nervous manner or help her to run the home as any normal woman might have done.

My daily life with the Donalds at this stage was grim. Everything – apart from my own little world out in the open air – seemed to be a problem. Food, heating, the amount of work I had to do, being treated as an idiot, constantly being reminded that I was not a 'proper' child of the family, that I was adopted. Even my footwear and clothing caused problems!

Chapter 8

Some childhood memories

Although life with the Donalds was grim, there were intervals when I had something other than survival to think about, when things were happening within the community – such as the Church Fete or Christmas celebrations – that I was allowed to play a part in or when I would get up to things that a normal young boy would have got up to.

For me Christmas at home was getting a letter from Father Christmas. It was written on a piece of brown paper with a burnt stick and explained that he had run out of toys and that he would see me next year. I knew, however that my foster brother and sister would get presents (although never a great deal of them). At least they would have had something. I understood that I didn't have any because I was less of a priority. This feeling of being inferior was ever-present. When it came to getting the firewood, if I made a suggestion that Molly or my foster brother could help a bit I would get a kick in the arse so hard that it would land me under the table. Either that or I would get a good beating from Arthur's belt – and the kind you wouldn't forget in a hurry. Once you got a bit of that you had no desire to argue, you just did whatever was required. The punishment was carried out without even thinking about it and that's just how it was. As a young boy, I didn't have any choice but to put up with it and then to make my escape to my sanctuary in the fields as soon as I could.

There were things that were traditional in the Church at Christmas. We would decorate the church for the festive season with all the seasonal flowers and when it was finished it was truly a sight to behold. Everyone chipped in at this time; my job was fetching and carrying. Some of the parishioners would bring all the different flowers available at that time of the year. Christmas would be the only time that many of our neighbours would want to do something for us. It was as if they had suddenly woken up, opened their eyes and seen us standing there hungry and dressed in rags. The people in the area who went to that church in Dunganstown would feel that they had a reason to spare a thought for us around Christmastime. We would have hampers with Christmas cakes and Christmas puddings. Some of the cakes that we would be given were wonderfully decorated with icing, little sugared beads and almond icing. They would be decorated to the highest standards and with professionalism beyond your wildest dreams. There were boxes of sweets and biscuits wrapped in Christmas paper, and we would have a wonderful time for a while. They obviously must have taken the view that by looking after us with these types of presents for the Christmas period they had done their duty as Christians. Of course, the main reason why they picked us out to give us cakes and hampers at Christmas was because we were doing church work. It brought us a bit more into their focus and they felt they were doing something for the poor of the parish.

Daisy would try to trade some of this stuff that we received at Christmas for food later on in the year with her various friends and connections. We didn't take too kindly to this at the time. I can see now, years later, why she did this.

Another annual church event was the garden fete that would take place every Whit Monday. Then there would be all types of games including Ludo, Aunt Sally, lucky dips and so on and for us kids it was a great occasion. For me, though, it was a two-edged sword. It not only gave me an event to enjoy but it also highlighted my poverty. My trousers had so many holes in them that I had to wear two pairs of trousers just to try and keep decent. I hoped the holes in one pair would not be in the same place as in the other pair. The parson's cousins, who visited from Dublin, used to make fun of me because of my trousers. They made fun of me not just because of the holes but also because Whit Monday would usually have been hot and they used to wonder why anyone would wear two pairs of trousers. They jeered, 'We thought country lads were supposed to be tough, so why wear two pairs of trousers?' and often my embarrassment would be just too much for me to bear. Overall, though, I enjoyed these fetes. There would be tents with tea and cakes. Of course, nobody in my family had money to waste on buying cakes but sometimes people who were visiting the fete would take me in and give me a cup a tea or a bun – but the locals would not help us. It was if they were ashamed of us and didn't want to be seen around us scumbags in rags. I suppose it's something that the middle class and upwards – the Church of Ireland people – were bred to do. They were able to accept a situation that was not going to be easy to address and they could set it aside, and as they say, a good soldier never looks back. In any civilised society there must surely be a duty to rescue those worse off than yourself and it fails me how they could never grasp this. It defies belief that people who are in a position to do something, do nothing to help. It is like seeing a person fall into a river and then standing, watching them drowning. Maybe I am not that type of person who can ignore a situation or person in need of help. I am the type of person that if somebody needed my help I would have no hesitation in giving it, but that's the way I am. Anyway, the tea tents at the church fetes seemed something amazing to me just to look at, but to actually be able to taste the cakes as well, well you'd never forget the experience.

The rectories where the church fetes were held often had small farms, and they were beautiful places with wonderful big lawns. It all changed when independence came. By the early 50's these events were very much in the decline. Ireland would have previously had influences of druid and then, later, Christianity. Irish customs and culture later began to get Anglican influences. Christianity brought its own demons – many people died for their beliefs – and along with Christianity came guilt. It was this legacy that was to influence the way that we unwanted children were treated by society in Ireland.

After the fetes I would have to return to my cold reality. Many nights I would rock myself to sleep thinking of some of the things that had happened to me so far. One of the things that came back to me at night was an incident that happened when we were at Barn Park. One of Arthur's greyhounds had a litter of pups, which he didn't want. I remember going into the yard to find these lovely little puppies trying to struggle out of the slurry pit into which they had been flung. It is amazing that not only did these memories come to me when I was sleeping in the Dunganstown schoolhouse, but also for many years after and they persist even now when I am over sixty years old. The horror has never gone away. Surely it couldn't have been right to do away with those pups in such an awful way. It really did haunt me to think of those poor little things struggling for air only to be pushed back in again to extinguish their lives.

Because we had gone back to the Dung-anstown schoolhouse to live, we were back doing the church work again. We had to scuffle the gravel, mow the grass in the graveyard, clean the church, polish the seats, and ring the bell. I had to blow the organ though really that was my foster father's job, but in actual fact he did it only very rarely. It always seemed that in the end I would have to do it and that's why there used to be rows with the churchwarden because they weren't very happy about it. Obviously they had good reason not to be happy because the first Sunday morning that Arthur should have been ringing the bell, I was left to do it. This was not a good idea as I had never rung a bell before and believe me it isn't as simple as you might think. Because I was small I could not get the continuity in the rope pulling. It was an awful experience. When I could only get the one tone from the ringing of the bell, the vicar came flying down from the pulpit, the church wardens came piling in, and it seemed everybody was set against me and I was terrified. The vicar was shout-ing 'my God they'll think there's a funeral, what on earth is going on?' At the same time the churchwardens were shouting 'out of the way, let me do it' and of course. I let them do it.

They managed to get another toll out of it but they only ended up with the same tone as me. In the end I reluctantly found myself back at it again and amazingly I got the thing going and found the knack. When you consider that I wasn't even eleven years old at this stage, it was a major task for a lad to have to do. It was a good job too that I got it going because if I hadn't we could well have been getting evicted again. We would have been heading for Daisy's, I've no doubt, only to experience another good session of rows over being there. Old Mrs Macdonald used to play the organ in the church. She was a very tidy, prim and proper lady you might say, but always very, very professional. She was an ex-schoolteacher and she didn't take fools lightly but she was very good at her job.

I remember one occasion when there was a wedding on (in fact it was one of Dick Reynolds's daughters who was getting married) and I was pumping the bellows for the organ. Suddenly I heard something snap and I had to go like the devil to keep the air to the right level. You see they used a weight on a string to mark the level to pull the bellows to. When the weight came to the level of the organ I had to keep the weight on that level and if I didn't it would cause the organist to go mad at me, When things weren't quite right she often thought that I had dozed off, but I hadn't on this occasion. In fact, one of the strings on the bellows had snapped. After a great deal of panicking and severe words she did accept that there was nothing that I could have done. It did mean though that I had to pump twenty times harder than normal and it was very clunky – not the sort of situation wanted in a church and certainly not at a wedding! There were a lot of very red faces in the church that day, though luckily it was the last hymn of the service and we got away with it. They soon got a specialist in to sort out the organ. So for me, to my enormous relief, it was back to scuffling the gravel outside and mowing the grass.

Mind you, mowing the grass took a great deal of skill as it was cut not with a lawn mower but with a scythe. To begin with, this job had to be done by an adult and it took a great deal of effort but in the end I too was able to cut the grass as if a lawnmower had done it, irrespective of how long or short it was. People used to marvel when I completed the mowing – so much so that some of the people would want me to do their gardens too. I used to tend the vicar's garden and would get a very good meal for doing it. The vicar's wife, Mrs Foster would bring me out the best of her homemade cakes and jam and a nice mug of tea. I was not used to this sort of treatment and I thought it was absolutely wonderful. On top of these treats I used to get a few bob for the job, all of which went towards a bit of bread on the table. When I returned home I then would have to go to Williams's little shop which wasn't too far away, or to Cole's which was three or so miles away or to Paddy Slatery's shop which was four or so miles away. If we had money, they would send me to the shops in all types of weather. I would go with a big sack and fetch the groceries. Some people would be allowed credit but we were on stop for any food on the slate in all of the shops because of all the bills that had been run up. This was always a big embarrassment to me. I would return with a sack full of groceries paid with the money for looking after the church, the sexton's pay and from Daisy's land letting money. You can imagine how hard it was to carry a big bag like this, particularly when there was snow on the road – six to nine inches sometimes – or driving rain and winds. I had to push a bike fully laden and for me as young kid it was a very tough task.

Bringing the shopping was not the only drudgery I had to endure in my young life. The farmers would often get me to do 'thinning'. The thinning of the turnips, mangle and beetroot meant being on my knees for long periods. The ground would be bone dry during the summer. Some of these clods of dirt were so hard that it felt like I was kneeling on razor blades. I would have an old sack around my knees and the sun burned me from the top. I earned about six pence for 100 metres – six pence in old money that is. When it was time to collect the money, I certainly knew that I had really earned all of it. While children of today could refuse such tasks, in those days children never argued – they just completed what was asked of them. We never even thought, 'Well, should I do it?' or 'Why am I doing it?' or even 'Why should I have to?'

After these hard tasks I would come home only to have to go out again to collect the wood, as nobody else would. If I didn't do it I knew that I would get a good hiding or go without a cup of tea or whatever else was going. That was what life was like for somebody who wasn't wanted. Life certainly wasn't a picnic for my foster siblings Molly and Sean either – in fact it was a horrendous experience for any child but at least they were loved. I think it was even worse for a child who wasn't loved – and knew it.

I used to help a lot of people in the area on the farms but, like any young child not brought up properly, I had my faults. I must have been a proper pain to some of the local people because of the tricks I got up to. I used to lie in wait for the Walker's tractor and pelt the guys on the tractor with cow muck or what ever I could get my hands on.

Obviously, they weren't very happy about it but it gave me a great deal of pleasure for whatever reason. Other times I would wait whilst men would be setting out to the fields for strip grazing and as soon as I saw poor old John Murphy putting the electric reel around his shoulders and walk well down the field with it then I would switch the electric on and watch while he did a version of the highland fling in the field. He would be cursing and swearing and he knew very well who had done it. But none of the men could catch me until one day when, unfortunately for me, they had had enough of my capers. Mick Walker grabbed me and he hung me over the back of the trailer by the arse of my trousers with my nose just skipping over the road as fast as the tractor was moving. It was an experience that I never wanted to go through again and it certainly cured me of getting up to those sorts of pranks. As they released me from the trailer I felt very lucky that I had survived to tell the tale.

I didn't annoy all the people in the area though and I was usually reckoned to be a good little worker. There was a man who kept the local shop, had the petrol pumps and who had an old Ford lorry that he used to deliver turf, coal and logs for customers. He also used to collect crockery from the Arklow crockery factory for delivery to customers in Dublin and so on. Now, I didn't know it at the time but this man had adopted two girls himself and obviously had some concern and understanding for what was happening to me. He sent word to me that he wanted me to help his driver do the deliveries. I worked for him a week but at the end of the week he told me that I would have to grow a bit before he could start me on again. What I didn't know at the time was that he expected me to be wearing long trousers but he was too embarrassed to make any comments on this. But, proving how concerned and sincere he was, after three months had passed he met me himself and said if I could find myself a pair of long trousers for the following Monday morning then I could have the job back. Unfortunately for me I was no further forward in resolving my trouser problem so I didn't go back to work for him. To be fair, even if I had sorted out the problem as he wished I would not have returned to work for him as I was still very upset from my previous experience but it shows you that you don't always know the reality of any situation and the true goodness of some people. This man was one of the very few people around who gave a damn about me and what I would become. The worse part about it is that I did not find out for many years the trouble this man was putting himself through just to help me

Like all young boys, I had accidents from time to time as I played or went about my business. One that I particularly remember involved one of the traps that my foster father had set that hadn't gone off properly. I noticed it as I walked down the cart road. The trap pan had actually frozen and was resisting the freedom of the spring of the trap to activate itself. I went to put this right but as an eleven year old I wasn't strong enough to keep it down. I had just about given up the idea of releasing the trap and had my hand about a foot away when suddenly the trap went off. My thumb was trapped in it – it wasn't a pleasant experience at all, especially on a freezing frosty morning. I started to run to Daisy's as fast as I could with my hand well and truly caught in the trap. As I got a bit nearer to the hill house with my arm tucked up to my chest, Daisy could see me from window and shouted 'Glory to god, what has the poor eejit got up to this time, what sort of an animal has he got?' I was always bringing something back – either it was birds or animals so Daisy assumed that I had a bird or a little animal in my arms. As I got nearer, however, she could see the blood on my hand and clothes and the terror on my face. She had the grim task of having to re- lease the trap, which had gone right through and crushed the bone of my thumb. As usual, they got the Jeyes fluid and hot water and a rag to clean the gruesome gash on my thumb.

I was working in the Dunganstown grave- yard one summer's day, it was about the time of the Queen's coronation, in fact, and this very posh, American-styled Hillman saloon pulled up outside. The people in the car were related to the Hoyes of Dunganstown – a family that had died out in our area a very long time ago, long before I was born. They had come to deal with their family's very large vault in the Churchyard. There were just two coffins in the vault though there was enough room in the remaining empty places to bury the whole of the population of Wicklow town itself. This vault was underground and there were steps leading down in to it. These people had travelled to Wicklow because they wanted to have the railings around the vault fixed so that it couldn't be opened up again. English scout groups would often come over to visit it and I know that some of them went down into the vault and opened up the old lead coffins to see if they could find anything. Obviously, these young lads did this out of curiosity and this would have been viewed as a very big adventure for them, but the family wanted to make sure that there was to be nobody else tormenting their relations so they had the vault made secure.

The Hoyes were at one time a very wealthy family who had strong connections in Ireland, and in Co. Wicklow in particular. They had emigrated to America but they still had a lot of investments all over Britain.

They asked my foster father and me to clean up the inside of the vault and take all of the weeds out. We did this work very quickly for them and they were so pleased with what we had done that they brought us a very large box of sweets and a lockable box with the Queen's photo, and also a photo of her and her husband. Mrs Hoye also brought each of us children a crown and a huge big coronation crown moneybox. These gifts were treasure indeed, especially as, living in Southern Ireland, you couldn't easily get the bits and pieces to do with the Queen's coronation as you could in the North or anywhere else. The family were very kind to us and I can still remember their gifts that we treasured for many years.

When I was a kid I used to rummage around in all the old trunks, boxes and cases. Daisy had postcards and letters from all over the world and they all had stamps. I had no idea of stamp values or any appreciation of the art of stamp collecting but somehow a lot of these stamps attracted my attention, so I decided I would cut them all off the letters and postcards. I made a book out of brown paper and then some glue with a little bit of flour and water. I stuck them in the book and when I had finished I had a huge collection of these stamps but no idea of the value. There was an English family living in one of the workers' bungalows by the name of Wadlow. One of the sons, who was about eleven was a serious collector of stamps. I showed him my stamps and he was gobsmacked with what he saw in the rough little book that I had made. He used to plague me to let him have them and he offered me ten shillings for them. I didn't particularly want to sell them, although I obviously had no idea of their true value. He never gave up and in the end he offered me £1.50 for the book. I couldn't believe it! I thought he had gone mad, as £1.50 was a lot of money to me. If he wanted them that badly, I thought, O.K. he can have them. To this day I still do not know whether I made a wise decision or not. The Wadlow family lived there for some time. Local gossip had it that when one of their grandparents died that they would be in for a lot of money. Lo and behold, they did die and they were left, as far as I know, a great deal of money. The parents left the children at home with one of their aunts to look after them, while they went on a very grand holiday in France. The family was struck by tragedy because whilst they were in France the big, posh hotel that they were staying in got burnt to the ground and both Mr and Mrs Wadlow lost their lives.

Very occasionally, there would be something that would break the monotony of work and hunger in my life. One such occasion was when a prominent local lady took us to the zoo. We rarely visited funfair events or zoos or what have you, so this was a real occasion for us. Mrs Walker plucked up the courage to take us three children to Dublin Zoo – even with our rags and in our smelly state. I'm sure it was an unforgettable experience for her. To us, however it was simply a marvellous adventure to see the animals from all of the wild places all over the world. There were elephants, lions, monkeys and all sorts of animals beyond our imagination. She only took us this once and nothing like it ever happened again. I imagine she thought, 'Well, I've done my good deed for God for I took them out for the day.' It was obviously an event for her as much as it was for us and I'm sure her very posh red Oxford car never had such a load of snotty-nosed, uncared for children in it either before or since.

Once in a while we would go to the seaside. We would have to walk about three miles but for us, of course, wherever we went it was all about walking and having to walk back up very great inclines. On hot days these walks were less pleasant, particularly when you are wearing old worn-out Wellington boots. In the summer these would stink like hell and most times we wouldn't have socks on but each foot wrapped up in a bit of old rag. One trick I learned at the seaside was to check the area where people got changed. Often I would find some loose change in the sand and once even a five-shilling piece! There used to be a man at Jack's Hole beach who would have a crate of pop for sale and he was sure of a visit from me if I struck lucky in the sand.

We made our own fun too from time to time. We would play up Daisy and May in various ways. We used to take the old pony that had been pensioned off from the Walker's farm inside Daisy's house. The pony proved to be a very, very tight fit. This pony was very docile and often would follow you if you held a bowl in front of him. This was how we got him into the house and Daisy would go mad when she found out what we had done, particularly as he did his 'business' on the table. That didn't go down at all well. This was one of the ways that we played Daisy and May up.

Daisy and May's Hill House farm was in a very attractive area and tourists used to come from Dublin to have a picnic. In those days, of course, you didn't have the same restriction on going on other people's property as you have today. Although there would be plenty of places with signs up saying 'No Trespassers' or 'Trespassers will be prosecuted', most people took no notice of them. My foster father and his mates used to have a trick they played to get their hands on the cakes and so on that the tourists brought for their picnics. They would get a mad Billy goat and aim it in the direction of where the people were having their picnic and then let go. Of course, most times the Dublin people (who often hadn't seen a goat up close) would flee like rabbits and leave their spread behind. My foster father and his mates would then gleefully have their pick of whatever they wished from the nicely laid out picnic.

The old parlour that Daisy and May had would, in its heyday, have been a lovely room, though we very rarely used it. It had a piano and a big long old settee. On top of the mantelpiece there were two big pottery Spaniel dogs with chains that looked magnificent. An English lady, Mrs Flint, repeatedly tried to buy these ornamental dogs from

145

Daisy. She wouldn't sell them at first, but Mrs Flint would wait until Daisy was in need of some money and then she would have another go at trying to get these dogs. She got them eventually and they left a very big gap in the poor old parlour. Daisy also had some very large seashells and she used to get us to put the shells to our ears so we could hear the roar of the sea in them.

The old Hill House farm building has now been left to go down hill and what a sad thing that is because in its day it would have been a fine place and a very lovely building. The parlour would have been a very homely family place to be in. The tunes played from that piano will always stick with me, no matter where I go.

Throughout these years that involved lots of pain and suffering there would always be these sorts of episodes and memories that would make me feel happy. Even so, when I went home at night I'd still wonder, and often be haunted by, that woman who was chasing my foster mother screaming for me to be given back to her. As I got older the need for me to find out who she was grew stronger and stronger.

Chapter 9

Meet the neighbours

Most of the people in the communities around us wherever we lived in my growing-up years were members of the Church of Ireland and were involved in farming in some way. I came into contact with them mostly through my doing odd jobs for them or sometimes, when I got on the wrong side of them because of some prank or other.

I recall working for one lady who was a great influence on me after my foster mother died. Her name was Mrs Heavener. I would go, together with my foster siblings, down to her house to get a meal and it would often be the only meal we would get for quite a few days. If she hadn't been around, God only knows what would have happened to us. Of course, we must have been a nightmare for her and her family as they weren't very rich people; they were just ordinary farmers. They themselves often struggled to make ends meet, but they were one of the few families who tolerated us. We spent many an hour down on their farm on Cullen Road. It was a lovely old farm place and they had an old crocked-out van which we would spend many hours sitting in and pretending that we were flying all over the place. They had a son called William, who was near my age. William was an absolute daredevil and he had nerves of steel. He would climb the highest tree he could find and hang out of it by his ankles. I remember him taking me on his bike and going down this hill and he said with his usual devilment 'I wonder what its like to ride a bike without having your hands on the handle bars and closing your eyes?' I was doomed to find out. We tumbled over and over and as we landed down in the ditch, I cracked my nose on his head. That was the sort of lad William was. He had an older brother who was called Digby – he was a terror as well. After Digby had shaved, he would wait and watch everyone coming into the yard and he would make sure he would chuck the shaving water out of the window at just the right time to catch him or her. It would land fairly and squarely on the head of the latest arrival in the yard. Needless to say, he would take great glee in achieving a direct hit. One day the boys' father was driving the tractor down the road with John Burke – from a neighbouring farm – sitting on the mudguard and Digby was out with his .22 rifle. He spotted poor old John on the mudguard of his father's tractor and he took aim and shot his hat off. Later I was to find out the effect that this shot had on John Burke.

They also had a sister called Lavender who was totally different from them. She was very prim and proper. She emigrated to England and ended up marrying a Scottish guy who was in the RAF. They went to Canada and a few years later the whole of the Heavener family emigrated there as well, which was a great loss to me. Charlie Heavener, the father, was a fellow who liked his beer and people reckoned he would drink himself out of business. Funny, but despite his business failings he never gave up and even when he lost his farm he would have another one within a week or so, and then soon be back to square one. He was the sort of chap who would borrow a tenner off a mate he met in the street and then spend that tenner on his mates in the pub. I suppose Mrs Heavener felt that it would be better if she could get him to Canada away from his drinking mates and the drinking. It was obviously a very serious problem with him and for the family as they had a son who was only a couple of years old and another, older son, called Dave. There was a large gap between him and the last child and I suppose she was hoping to get away from the drudgery that she had gone through all of her life, together with the hardships caused by the old drink.

One time I was at the Heavener's new farm down in Castletimen (this was the last farm they had before they emigrated to Canada) and I could see the sky was getting very dark. A very serious storm appeared to be brewing and I think that by now Mrs Heavener had had enough of me and wanted me to go. I didn't really realise this was what she wanted and I suggested staying because of the storm brewing. She began to imply that I was a bit of a sissy worrying about the weather. I was a bit insulted by this and tried to defend myself against the accusation, 'no, I think there's going to be a really bad storm.' 'Oh,' she said, 'you're a big girl's blouse'. However, in the end she relented and brought me indoors. We were sitting in the kitchen when the storm broke and there was the most horrendous crash, bang, wallop of thunder and next thing a light shot across the house following all the stainless steel pipes in the airing cupboard.

Mrs Heavener grabbed her newborn son and me and went into the bedroom where we waited for the storm to stop. She shook like a lily and I'm pleased to report that she never said anything to me again about being frightened of thunder. I wasn't really fearful of thunder as I often spent time on the hills when thunder broke and while it wasn't a pleasant experience I usually stayed out there. Even as a child I could read the signs in the sky as if it was a map and so I knew without doubt when thunder was on its way. In actual fact, what I was wary of was getting wet. As a child I suffered greatly with a fever flu, which would have been the result of the neglect I experienced throughout my childhood, especially when I was in the Bethany home. As a consequence, I tried to avoid getting wet if I could because it could result in me getting this flu-like fever. When I did get it, the result was often that I passed out. Sometimes I would be found anywhere on the hills, passed out completely. I would rarely receive any doctor's treatment or anything like that for this complaint. In those days children like us rarely gave into illness. It was just a fact of life.

Another family that played an important – and ever-present – part in my childhood was the Walker family. I was to find out much later in my life that Mrs Walker was, in fact, a signatory (along with Reverend Foster) to the fostering arrangements made by the Bethany Home with the Donalds. She would never have been far away from our antics one way or another as I would often go down to their farm and help out John Murphy, their cowman and general farmhand. We were always popping in and out of their yard and I'm sure there would have been many a time when Mrs Walker would have dreaded the very sight of us but there was also a positive side because I would help down on the farm in all aspects of their operations.

Mrs Walker one day told us that if we wanted some apples from the orchard we could help ourselves to the ones that were on the ground. Now, this was a pretty big deal for us. So we gathered a load of these apples from off the ground and everything was going great and we were pleased as Punch at our good fortune, but then Molly spotted a big, shiny red apple way up in the tree – the one that you always want. Molly climbed up the tree to get the apple and the next thing we heard a loud squawk coming from the house. Mrs Walker stood at the door waving her arms and shouting at us to get out of the tree and out of the orchard altogether – immediately. She reminded us that she had specifically told us not to go up the tree to pick any of the apples and only to take those ones that lay on the ground. This meant that our apple picking had come to abrupt end and we were so disappointed. We knew that Molly had stepped out of line but we couldn't really understand the problem. We knew that at least ninety percent of those apples in the tree would never be picked by the Walkers and they would all end up on the ground anyway.

As you can probably tell from this, Molly was quite a tearaway. We had a big white Billy goat; he was a lovely looking animal and looked like a young pony. Molly would catch the poor old Billy goat and would try to ride him as if he was in the Grand National. He didn't like this and eventually he started getting wise to this business so he used to get up to speed and then tip his head and Molly would, of course, go right over the top and onto the ground. I can tell you though, she was a great horse rider; she would get up on any animal and ride them as if she had the full saddle and stirrups on. Nothing would have freaked her and she appeared fearless. But it did get us into the odd scrape or two – like with the Walkers' apples.

The Walkers were not your ordinary run-of-the-mill type farmers; they would be your gentleman' type of farmers. It was as if they farmed just for a bit of fun. It didn't really seem to matter to them whether their farm was a success or a failure as they made most of their income as glasshouse tomato growers in Guernsey. They were known back in the 1950s as multi-millionaires. All of their children went to boarding schools and, for their youngest son Colin, they employed a girl to take him out in his pram at six o'clock in the morning. He would have to be pushed across the hills every day and it wouldn't matter what the weather was like; it was obviously their aim to get fresh air in to his lungs, which, they believed, would help him in his future life. That was the sort of thing that they could afford to do.

There were some very prominent people around this area. A family called Malalous had lived in the old Cedars house before the Walkers bought it. Mr Malalous was a Scotsman and he was well-known locally for riding horses while wearing a kilt. He lived in Dunganstown, Co. Wicklow throughout the war years and had a very comfortable life while he lived there, though he eventually returned to Scotland and then in the great Labour landslide victory he was elected to Parliament.

Malalous wasn't the only famous politician who had lived in the area. Across the way in Avoca, the great Parnell had lived. Like many of the locals, Parnell knew how to communicate. In his day, Parnell would have been known in the four corners of the world for being able to command vast crowds with his rousing speeches. Today radios and televisions are used to compensate for modern politicians' lack of the types of skills that he had. You can imagine him setting off in his horse-drawn carriage, on his way to Dublin and then off to the Houses of Parliament in London. He was someone who was very much admired and respected, even by the opposition, because of his professionalism and skill. His sheer, natural ability of communicating with people captivated crowds easily and totally. I would daydream about these important events and people in Irish history as sort of a break away from my own troubles.

Of course, not everyone who lived in the area was rich or famous – far from it! But what some of the locals lacked in money and property, they more than made up for in character. In those days everybody did a lot more talking to each other and there were always tales to tell. Two old gentlemen, William McDonald and Fred Lofter, would sit and talk on Sundays after the church service and the tales would flow thick and fast. The walk up Cavan's Lane to the schoolhouse was very steep and they would sit on the steps at the gateway having a good old chat about everything that had gone on during the week. Fred would then get on his bike and cycle up to Cullen and his dinner would be ready when he got in. By the time William had walked back down Cavan's Lane his dinner would also be ready for him.

William McDonald always used to make the point that he was born on the same day as the launch of one of the big newspapers in Britain. He was strangely proud of the fact that his birthday was on the same day as such an important event. He was a remarkable man, even at eighty years of age he would have all the cows in ready to be milked, all the udders washed, in no time at all. Henry, his son, would spend a lot of his time talking to me at the end of the day whenever he had the chance. He would talk to me about lots of things – the fields that he was ploughing, the day the Second World War broke out and the fact that his old Alice Chambers tractor was still going as good as the day it was bought.

Murphy was another character in the area. He had lost an eye while cutting a hedge. He loved his Porter and he loved wakes. In those days in Ireland they had the custom of the wake. This was held when somebody dies and usually resulted in three days and three nights of drinking plenty of Porter and eating the best of food. Everybody who knew the person that had died would bring beer, mutton or lamb, bacon or beef. You would have to bring something so that the people who were having the wake didn't have to provide for the wake. People who knew Murphy would ask 'what's the matter with you?' if he wasn't looking as perky as normal and he would reply, 'ah see, Jesus there hasn't been a wake for a fortnight.' He'd be well put out because of that, as often this would mean he hadn't had a drink. When he went to a wake he would binge on the beer and he would be quite happy with the result.

When people got together to chat it was inevitable that ghost stories were passed around and in that part of Ireland there was a great deal of ghost stories. I was told many times that before they had electricity in the church the old furnaces for the boiler had to be lit in the afternoon and stoked up at midnight so that the church would be warm for Sunday morning. This always presented a bit of a problem because you would have to go down in the middle of the night, through the graveyard and into the church, which wasn't a pleasant experience for anybody. Anyone doing this would be all freaked out by the time they had finished stoking the furnace. This chore was normally carried out by my foster father and my foster aunts, who were never really worried about ghosts. There was, however, a period when they didn't carry out this duty and one of Dick Reynolds's brothers from Dublin, Cecil Reynolds, had to take on that responsibility on to cover for a while. He was on his way into the churchyard to get it all fired up for the next Sunday morning service and as he got into the churchyard and headed towards the door he saw what he assumed to be a ghost sitting on the stile. He stared for a few seconds at this ghostly apparition in front of him, then left the church as fast as his legs could carry him. To this day he has no idea as to whether he made his rapid exit over the stile entrance or over the gateway but all he

158

knew is that he would not be lighting the fire that night. The next morning they had a very cold church and there was a lot of muttering and moaning.

Another story involved a doctor who once lived in Cavan's Lane. It is said that he fell over when he was drunk one night and drowned in a puddle of water and the story has it that you could see his ghost standing at the end of the gateway as you went by at a certain time of night. We used to have to go up and down Cavan's Lane quite regularly. It became a habit for most locals that they would be making sure that they had a good look over their shoulders when they went past this point to make sure that no strangers were accompanying them.

The story of the doctor's death was the sort of tale that was very common and there were other roads in the area with similar stories. Down near Sheep Hill, a hen with a clutch of chickens could be seen crossing the road as midnight struck, night after night. On other roads there would be reports of hearing carriages and horses clip-clopping along at certain times of night. Even those who said they didn't believe any of these tales were always very careful in these areas. Let's be fair, all of us locals were exposed to these stories from a very young age so we took it pretty seriously. We would all play it a bit safe and take precautions – just in case the stories were true. There was an ash tree down Cullen Road that was old and very gnarled – it was all grown into itself in loops and they reckon that whenever a member of the Burke family died, a banshee used to be in that tree, whining away. It was said she had very long, grey hair and she would sit and comb it endlessly. The banshee would let out a screech that would make you freeze into a block of ice if you heard it.

One peculiar story that particularly stuck in my mind involved a lady from a very rich family in Tipperary who had died from the Black Plague. She was duly buried in the family vault but was not allowed to rest in peace. The family's butler crept back to the vault after the funeral, opened the lead coffin and attempted to remove the woman's rings. He struggled with this so much that he eventually decided to cut her fingers off to get at the rings. The blood flowed and, according to the tale, this profuse bleeding caused the woman's circulation to restart and she came back to life. (Apparently it was quite common for people to be buried while they were merely in a coma or unconscious). As she sat up in her coffin, the butler took off as fast as he could. The lady eventually managed to get out of the coffin and made her way to the grand entrance to her home. Hearing her distinctive knock, her family knew that by some miracle she had returned. She stood on the doorstep, trying to stem the flow of blood from her fingers. The family, of course, welcomed her back. The butler was never seen or heard of again.

The ghostly experiences that were talked about in those days go on and on. There is the tale of the Conway's place at the back of Daisy's Hill House, that during the black flu of 1919, ten of the children in the family died of the flu. People went to the wake on foot as they did in those days and they would walk across the hills to take short cuts. After the wake, one of the mourners had been given a leg of mutton to take back to his family because the grieving family had been given more food than they needed for the wake. As he made his way back across the hills, he reckoned something kept lapping up around his legs and he just could not get shut of it and by the time he got home he was in a lather of sweat and was in a great state of shock. His family reckoned the meat that he had with him was rotten and there was a horrendous stench coming from it although the animal had been killed just that morning. Nobody could offer any explanations as to what he had experienced. Whatever the truth of the matter, it was a question that nobody had the answer to.

Daisy's brothers were also tormented by ghostly happenings. In an effort to save up for their emigration to Canada they worked very hard. They invested in the first horse drawn hay moor and they also drew quarry stone by horse and cart to extend the Wicklow pier for shipping and for breaking the force of the tide to prevent flooding in the Wicklow town. They once used this cart to help to mow crop circles into a field. They worked all through the night on this and it was said that they cut some of the circles with their new modern machinery. They were badly tormented all night and it is said that when they went home to sleep the furniture in the house was moving on its own all over the place. There was certainly no shortage of ghost stories in the area – it seemed that everyone had their tales to tell.

A few of the neighbours that I did a bit of work for would treat me well. When I took old Mrs Leonard's cows down to the fields for grazing, she would always meet me with a piping hot cup of tea and a very large buttered jam sandwich. Apart from the tea and the sandwich, the thing I remember most vividly about Mrs Leonard was her cats. She loved her cats to such an extent that some of her neighbours were not best pleased with her. Many thought she spoilt her own cats and sometimes her neighbours' cats as well. If you went to her house in the summer you would find cats laid out in the sun everywhere. I remember that her driveway from the road was lined on each side with the old balls from the fishing nets of years gone by. She was a wonderful old lady who raised her family on her own as her husband had been killed in the last week of the first world war. When you go around Ireland it is amazing how many people's lives were wrecked by those two great world wars.

Other characters in the area didn't play such an important part in my life but, nevertheless, they have remained in my mind. There was some guy whose farm up in Glen Healey was taken over by the forestry. He was known locally as the sort of bloke that, as far as anybody was concerned, was never bothered by women. He would always publicly make the point that he could manage life better without them. When the forestry workers were putting in new drainage systems on his land for the tree planting, they had to go through an old stone wall and here they found several old sweet cans stuffed with love letters from his many girlfriends. Needless to say he became the talk of the town.

There was another episode involving the forestry workers. One of the lads, who was in his late teens to early twenties, took Colonel Clark's left-hand drive American car for a midnight ride. It was in all of the local papers and was the big news of the day. In contrast to today's society where car theft (or joy-riding as it is known) is commonplace and the newspapers barely waste a sentence or two on such an incident; then everybody gasped at such an event. When the colonel would drive around in this big American car, it could hardly fit down the old lanes of Wicklow and Dunganstown; it actually filled the whole road and the bushes touched both sides of the car. As it passed through everybody constantly appeared to be very excited at the prospect of seeing the Colonel driving his car around. So when someone took his car out for a midnight ride it went down very badly. The poor lad ended up in jail.

All of these people played a part in my childhood – whether it was the work they gave me, the occasional food they gave me or the entertainment that their antics supplied. Sadly they have all passed on. Most of the farms that were owned by these people have now also all gone or are now owned by rich, foreign people. The area of Ireland that formed the beautiful backdrop to my childhood is now considered to be a millionaires' belt. The sad part of it all is not just that they've all gone but that their customs of hospitality and cheerfulness have also disappeared. No longer can you knock on somebody's door only to find a cup of tea waiting for you as quickly as you arrived.

Chapter 10

A mother's death

Looking back my childhood must have been a terribly difficult time for my foster mother although, at the time, I didn't appreciate it. She was always thin and physically weak and had a difficult job on her hands to raise children and keep a home going with very little money coming in even at the best of times. She eventually contracted TB and was placed in the Rathdrum sanatorium, which was especially for the treatment of people with this terrible disease. We children would occasionally walk to Rathdrum to see her in the sanatorium and I remember on one such visit she had made a box for her daughter Molly. This was for her to keep her girlie knick-knacks in and was beautifully made with gold stitching and edging. It was diamond shaped with a stiff plastic facing and the top had a sewn hinge. It surprised me that she could do such intricate work, even when she was so obviously ill.

Unfortunately there was very little they could do for people with TB in Ireland in those days so she was sent home to die in the crudest way possible in terms of proper medical help. There was nothing available to help us to keep her as comfortable as possible in this horrendous state. There was very little medical treatment given to her from the day the hospital dumped her at Daisy's house on the hill when the doctors had decided that they could not cure her dreadful condition. I still remember the night she died. Some of the local people such as Mrs Charlie Heavener visited and of course Reverend Foster visited her on that awful night so that she could make peace with her God.

Tuberculosis was one of the biggest killers in Ireland at that time but nobody from the Department of Health – or other officialdom – came to check up on the situation. It also had an inevitable affect on our schooling, as nobody wanted to sit near us. It emerged later that actually all the children in the school were told by their parents not to sit anywhere near us. To be fair about it, nobody would want to sit near me anyway because I was in rags and the rags were hardly ever washed (and neither was I!) so I must have been extremely unpleasant to be near. Any clothes that I had I would wear until they fell apart. Daisy would try to find somebody that had some second hand clothes to give her. I used to have an old pair of braces but the buttons had come off long before I got them so I used bits of wood to hold the braces onto the trousers. The trousers themselves were full of holes. These holes caused me great embarrassment throughout my childhood. Getting any clothes at all was a hard task for Daisy so she didn't worry too much about how well fitting they were. The clothes were often too big or too small but we had to put up with what we received.

Thinking about Kathleen's terrible death, all the memories come flooding back. No matter how much I try to bring positive thoughts about that time to mind, I'm left with bad memories of my foster mother – the time when she treated the dog bite on my arm with Jeyes fluid, hot water and bit of rag. She didn't carry out this task like a normal mother would – with tender loving care – but just as a necessity and then she sent me on my way without that little hug of affection that always goes with you when you have true love with your blood mother. My worst memory of my foster mother, Kathleen

Donald, is of her sifting in Daisy's house with her back to the window, the light was coming in, the rays from the sun shining across the room, with Molly on one knee and Sean, her new son, on the other knee. She was cuddling and loving them and telling me 'these are my real children. You are not. I can always take you back to the home that I got you from in Dublin!' Those memories, those words, they cut through you like a knife through butter. I suppose that this has stuck with me because of the pain. A child of eight or so would find that so hurtful, and so destructive that it leaves a scar that you will always carry and of course, to a child none of it could ever make sense. I suppose people who haven't experienced this sort of rejection would simply say 'Just sweep it aside. You're making too much of it' but when you're a little fellow life just doesn't seem to be that simple.

Another awful memory of the times when Kathleen was dying with TB was when she didn't want to finish her meal and tried to make me eat it. Knowing that she had a very contagious disease, you probably find it hard to believe that she would do this. For some unknown reason – I'm sure I didn't fully understand her illness at this time – something always told me that I should not eat it and I never did. Of course, it wasn't as easy as just refusing to eat it. One part of you thinks that you should eat it because she wants you to eat it, it would make her feel better, but another part of you is telling you it would be quite mad to eat this because of the fear of getting the disease. So, with all of this turmoil going around in my head, life was never easy. I would wonder if she was giving me the food because she hated me and I would ask myself 'is she doing this nasty thing because I wet the bed?' That was always a big worry of mine. I know now, of course, that when a child has gone through what I've been through there are emotional problems which are not made better by the way some people deal with them. If they wet the bed they need assistance not brutality. Being told that they are a dunce or an eejit will not help. I have tried to analyse why I was picked out to go through this caper and how my foster mother could have done some of the things that she did. Maybe it was because of her own hopelessness – the continuous fight against the impossible, knowing that she should never have adopted me in the first place.

I can still remember the Gardai visiting Daisy's to find out why I hadn't been going to school and Kathleen explaining to him that it was because she didn't have any clothes to send me in. The Gardai replied 'Well, you got this and you got that and you would have an allowance from him as he is adopted.' I can vividly remember her saying to him that she never had a penny from me through the adoption. The reason she gave was that it would have left my people in a position where they could come and take me back at anytime of their choosing. So, there seems to always be a contradiction running through the whole situation with Kathleen.

These cruel episodes stick in my mind. They are the experiences that I have endured. I suppose it's difficult to comprehend just how such cruelty took place with children who were taken into other people's families i.e. orphans or unwanted children. In my case I was given to a very, very, very poor family that was already in a totally hopeless situation – a non-winnable situation. It had been long established that Kathleen's husband was never going to provide in a sensible, coherent, logical way for her and her family. This, added to where she had come from and the religious nightmare that she was living, results in an abnormal situation in anybody's book. She would never have money in her purse to be able to spend on food and clothes and the bare necessities for herself and the family. I have no doubt in my mind that with money available – even a limited amount – she would have been a different person. I'm happy at this distance to be able to give her the benefit of the doubt. This is despite all the cruel things she did to me and the lack of care and affection that I suffered from plus an incredible incident that I remember happened one Christmas. We were, as usual, starving but she was given a huge white goose for Christmas. For some reason that I was never to discover, she did nothing with it except to eventually dump it out in the longest and tallest nettles in the wildest part of the garden. What happened was that after she had been given the substantial bird, it was laid on the table and there it stayed for a considerable time. Later in the year I was down at the bottom of the garden. It was extremely overgrown with nettles, bushes and briars and I came across the old white goose. It didn't make any sense to me. We had often gone hungry and to think that that big plump goose was down there, rotting away. It would have made a wonderful meal, as it was enormous. Well to me it was a bird, and not to make use of it, to me, given the circumstances, it just didn't seem to add up. So now you can see that when I say that they weren't bad people they were just incapable and incompetent and that – rather than wickedness – is what I am able to forgive them.

After my foster mother died we children were left pretty much to our own devices and we ran completely wild. We made our own life in every respect. Whatever degree of holding things together that my foster father had appeared to have before my foster mother died vanished. It seemed that he truly lost the plot after her death and, of course, now that his wife had died there was no one there between him and us children so we frequently had to bear the brunt of his moods. If he took up temporary work operating a thrasher machine, we wouldn't see him for a couple of weeks. He would earn a few bob only to drink it all in the pub later so that meant we didn't see any of it. As children we were totally neglected and abandoned by any adults. Our Great Aunts Daisy and May would only occasionally come down and see us but we would go up to see them quite often just to see if they had anything for us to eat or anything we could bring back with us. Mostly, however we fended for ourselves. We would come back after being out all day up in the hills or wherever and go back to a house that had no modern lighting; we would only have the light from the fire. We didn't even have money to buy paraffin for the lamps.

When you think there were three young children living in the old school house very largely on their own, in a house that had by this time long passed suitable for humans to live in, it was surprising that we still seemed to have escaped the notice of the local community. The upstairs rooms were riddled with woodworm. You would have to be very careful where you put your feet, as my foster sister found out when she went through the ceiling and was only saved by her arms as they caught her on the joists. There was always panic during the very big storms, with the house rattling and the very big weathercock whistling around at high speed on the roof. On odd occasions we would disturb a very large rat or two – which was never a very pleasant experience.

The house held its own dangers apart from its state of repair and the fact that we were alone. We had a very large beehive in the roof that had been there for many years.

I made some holes through the ceiling to it and I had buckets below catching the honey. That sounds very good, I'm sure, but there is a price to be paid for everything. In one year alone I got stung sixty-eight times – some people believe that eight stings from bees at the same time would kill a horse.

If the fabric of the house gave cause for concern, the sparseness and condition of the furnishings were even more desperate. I remember that we were out at the beach one day and when we got back, the makeshift table that took pride of place in the downstairs room was in a heap on the floor with its contents strewn around the room. We thought someone had been into our house causing trouble and damage while we were out (we never considered burglars, of course, as we knew there was nothing to steal). This table had been held up by a lump of wood tacked to the wall and had just one leg at the front so it must have been pretty rickety but it never dawned on us that the structure of the table could be at fault!

There were two rooms downstairs at the old schoolhouse but we only ever used one. This was our kitchen and dining room. The other downstairs room was the room where I kept the turkeys. This obviously caused a great deal of concern with the churchwardens when they found out about it, but to us we could see no reason for the fuss – despite the smell! It just shows how far away we were from being part of the civilized community.

Another problem we had with our houses – the schoolhouse or wherever we lived – was fleas. The beds were always infested with them as were our clothes and hair. You only had to have a quick look and you would be able to see fleas nestling in the folds of our clothing – under a collar for example or jumping from one place to another and it must have been obvious to anyone who had the misfortune to have to get close to us that we were flea-ridden. I was bitten terribly (the bites came up as great red lumps and sometimes even drew blood) and the fleas bothered me greatly. They pestered me and pestered me and I hated it. To this day, I am super-sensitive to fleas and am unable to have a cat for this reason.

On the occasions when my foster father was at home, if a tramp knocked on the door late at night he would have no hesitation in letting him stay the night. He did have a very big heart in these matters. Unfortunately, it would not be uncommon for us to find a pool of water on the floor and the tramp gone before we got up in the morning. These poor souls would be drinking methylated spirits, which was a very sad affair all round. Despite their poor state, we never felt that we were in any danger from letting these people share our home for the night.

After her mother's death in such awful circumstances and being left pretty much to our own devices, I suppose that the strain of the situation we were living in started to take hold with Molly. She began to get a taste for the nightlife and the lads. This had an effect on my relationship with her because she was always after any small amount of money that I had earned from my odd jobs. I would hide the few coins that I would earn from here and there in the hope of saving up enough money to buy myself a brand new pair of long trousers. That was one of the main ambitions that I had at that time. Not very adventurous, it's true, but it was so important to me then. However, it didn't matter where I hid the money, Molly would always end up finding it and then she'd be off to the fair. She wouldn't return until quite late and if my foster father were around it would wind him up something rotten. He would be so mad that he would be stalking around the house, shouting and screaming for her return working himself up into a right lather. All the time this mayhem was going on at home, Molly would be with some of the lads a few miles away. Sometimes you could hear them talking outside on a quiet evening and that would wind him up even more, as it often would be about two or three in the morning. These developments made me start to think about things I had never even considered before – like relationships. Even though I was only Molly's foster brother rather than a blood relative, I think we still would have died for each other – and no questions asked. Despite the fact that the family treated me differently and always used me for their best advantage, I still felt that I would do anything for them. Prior to those later years of adolescence there was no question that Molly and I could not have been closer even if we had been blood brother and sister. Molly however, was always very mindful that I never was her brother and never would be her true blood brother. But I was the brother who had accompanied her through this ordeal and that brother could not be any closer than a blood brother of any description that you might find.

In a sense all three of us children were abandoned in different ways. We were dumped by society, neglected, and often shunned and no one gave a damn. If you think about it Molly was a young girl growing up without her mother to tell her of the worldly affairs of life and to tell her how to cope with all of it. She had to get in to an apron and be the head of the house and try to be a mother to the family. She had no help from anyone to assist her in achieving this almost impossible task. This was to affect the rest of her life and, when she had a family of her own, the affect was to be passed on down the generations. The women in the lives of us children after my foster mother had gone found it hard to give love. Daisy and May didn't show me love, they would never hug me or even tap me on the head as a sign of affection. In their own little way they were the most wonderful people that could ever have lived because they did all they could to help us survive in those horrendous years of growing up. Sadly we didn't realise until many, many years later just how great they were. Daisy and May would give their last penny to help us. They gave their all, they shared the same crust of bread with us children, but God forgive us, we didn't appreciate it at the time. We played them up something terrible and that we can't deny, but they appeared to take it into their stride though they weren't young women when we came onto the scene. They were in their sixties by the time we were growing up and it must have been hard for them to cope with young children. I am now finding out for myself how tiring taking care of young children can be for an older person now that I have my own grandchildren.

I suppose a year or so before my foster mother died and for some years afterwards, my foster brother, foster sister and myself were close in that we were fighting the same battle – for survival. We would work out the best ways of getting stuff so that we could eat. We couldn't depend on my foster father at that time, as he would only work occasionally, whether it was forestry work or casual work on the farms or during the thrashing season. My foster father acted as if he had no ties in his life somehow, as he would just go off on his own for weeks, particularly during the thrashing period. Back at home he left three children who were running wild and who were having to look after themselves. When you look back there must have been something very wrong with society to allow this to happen. I remember some people complaining to him about us running wild and being pains in the neck to everybody. They suggested that we should be taken away where we could have been looked after properly. His reply was very simple, 'If you can catch them, you're very welcome to them.' That was his way of dealing with things. By the time my foster mother died he seemed to have lost any logic in his thinking and did not seem to be in the real world.

Whatever the reason was for all that befell us after my foster mother's death, there was no doubt that things deteriorated drastically from that point. Life certainly hadn't been easy before her death, but it was a whole lot worse after it.

Chapter 11

Introduction to Boxing

One of the most unlikely – but ultimately rewarding – experiences that I had to deal with in my youth was taking up amateur boxing, which my foster father was hell bent on my doing. Even now, I have not got the faintest idea why he wanted me to do this and it was certainly a complete mystery to me at the time. I definitely was not built for it because I was a half starved, uncared for and poorly clothed child. I certainly didn't have any strength or stamina to spare. None of that, however, mattered to him and he would normally get his way when he made his mind up that he wanted me to do something.

The boxing 'bug' seemed to bite Arthur Donald while he was with his mates, James O'Brien or the Hughes family. When he was at a loose end, my foster father would often go down to the O'Brien's or to the Hughes' place. He would sit around the fire with John O'Brien who used to work on the forestry but now had plenty of time for a chat with Arthur as, unfortunately he had had an accident where he fell down a gorge and hurt his back. He was on sticks for years. He had a huge family and, because of his accident, poor old Mrs O'Brien had to work like a slave to keep everything going and she certainly worked hard on the farm – she was as good as four men. They had a small land-commissioned farm and kept pigs, hens, and turkeys plus cows for milk. One of their sons (they had nine children) was Mick O'Brien who was not far off my age and he was selected as my first boxing challenge.

His father and my foster father were only too keen to get us to spar and box. They both loved boxing and knew a lot about it. Like a lot of people who never take part in the sport, they thought they knew more than even the most experienced boxers. We would have to have handfuls of grass instead of boxing gloves as this was supposed to ease the pain of the punch. Mick wasn't any keener on doing this than I was but he was offered a ten shilling note if he could come out on top in the fight with me, whereas I had to do it simply because Arthur had ordered me to. Whatever the rewards on offer, we both knew that we would have to fight until one of us gave up. I was only about twelve at this time and was far from in the peak of health and, now that I look back on it, it didn't make any sense to put me in this position although I did have a slight advantage as I was a bit older. It seemed to me that they used these fights to boost their own egos. They were living their ambitions out through us.

Fortunately for me and unfortunately for Mick, I caught him on the nose with a left jab. His nose began spilling blood and that ended the scrap. Mick's father went absolutely mad at him for him having to stop the fight because, you see, before we started there was a bet of five shillings on the outcome. Then Mrs O'Brien came to us in a flap saying 'Mother of God, what are you two grown men doing letting these two lads do this. It's uncivilized; you should be ashamed of yourselves. Haven't you got anything better to do with your time?' James O'Brien, however, was upset because his son hadn't come out on top and he had lost the bet. He was ready to give Mick another good hiding with his stick because he had let the side down. By the end of it all I don't know which was the worse fight, the fight I had with the lad or the row that took place afterwards. Of course, my foster father was quietly very pleased.

I never figured out why my foster father would insist on me boxing. I could only imagine that if I were to do better than the other kids he would have some pride in me. When you think of the courage a half-starved kid needed to take up such a sport, knowing that any confidence that he may have had had surely already been beaten out of him. Needless to say, my foster father would never listen to any excuses, especially when he heard that there was a club in Wicklow called Marian Boys Club where I could take part in some boxing. He immediately decided that I had to go there although we didn't know that he was short of one vital piece of information – nobody had told him that this boxing club was a Catholic one. It was a boys club founded in 1954 to give boys in the area who had just left school somewhere to go and something to do. The priest – Father Hans – who had founded this club and also ran it was an inspirational character who cared deeply about the community and succeeded, where many had failed, in overcoming the insular nature of the townspeople and in directing the energies of the boys of Wicklow.

On my first night's attendance at the Marian Club I was a small country lad dressed in rags and I was the joke of the night as I stood near the doorway. One clever clogs swung a large punch bag in my direction but I managed to duck to get out of the way. I was then told I had to spar with a local lad who, unlike me, knew his way around a ring. He tore into me and gave me a lesson in what it was like to be up against someone who knew their trade. It was a terrifying experience and as he hit me repeatedly, I didn't seem able to offer much of a defence. I will never forget the smell of the sweaty leather of the gloves. I really thought that my boxing days were going to end almost before they had begun, although I still did not know how I could tell my foster father that this boxing business wasn't for me. I wasn't sure which was going to be worse, getting battered or telling him that I was not going to do him proud. Somehow or another, I turned up for the next training night that came up. I will never know how I plucked up the courage to face this onslaught again. One of the problems was that in this club for about half of the time there would be nobody available to train the lads. This would result in the older and bigger lads trying to test their skills on the new lads and show them how good they were. I persevered with the boxing and attended regularly but I decided straight away that I would not try to take these lads out.

I had my adventures on my way to the boxing club as well as when I got there. To get to the boxing club I had to ride nearly six miles into Wicklow on my clapped out push-bike (with dodgy lights!), so to me it didn't make any sense at all to go there. I had the cold, dark nights to contend with too as I would always have to go in the middle of winter because the boxing season started at the end of September. Going into Wicklow town and meeting more lads in one night than I would normally see in twelve months out in the country was a pretty daunting task for me. I was more used to spending time with goats and other animals than I would be to meeting people. Also I was only dressed in rags and short trousers, which gave them all another excuse to take the Mickey out of me. I became a proper Aunt Sally for their entertainment and they had a great deal of pleasure out of messing me about.

I was riding my bike to the boxing club in Wicklow one night, and I was very mindful that my bike light didn't have a bulb as I was going to be cycling near where a Garda by the name of Lewan lived. He had a fierce reputation for summonsing people all around him without too much bother. He would often summons the local farmers for using their tractors and trailers for fetching fertilizer from the Wicklow harbour. They would pay agricultural road tax on their tractors, however as far as the Garda was concerned they should have been paying haulage tax rates if they wanted to ferry loads backwards and forwards on the main roads. Of course, they knew the risk they were running and some of these farmers took a lot of trouble to avoid his book by taking detours down small lanes. The Garda and his bike would catch up with them irrespective of their efforts. He certainly wasn't a man to mess with and the more I thought about not having a lamp bulb the more I was sure I would run into him before the night was out. Sure enough as I got to the town I spotted him, as large as life, and it was too late for me to take another route. I had no choice but to bite the bullet. I went up to him and laid my cards on the table, I told him I needed to borrow the price of a lamp bulb as my one had gone out on the way in. I informed him that my Aunt Daisy would pay him back when she was next in town. I believe the price of the bulb was about nine pence at the time but he hadn't got nine pence in change on him. To my amazement he said. 'You might as well borrow the shilling and then she can give me a bob when I see her.' I was taken aback and thought 'Bloody hell that wasn't so bad! Maybe he isn't as bad as everyone was saying.' However, I had relaxed too soon, as I only had gone up the road a few yards when he called me back. 'Where is your back light?' Thinking quickly, I replied, 'There's aluminium paint instead.' This didn't take him in for a second and he shouted at me, 'That's not worth a damn. Get a bulb for your lamp and get your Aunt Daisy to get you a proper rear light for a bike.' When I told everyone at home and at the boxing club, all about him giving me the shilling, no one could believe it. They were falling over laughing because the encounters that other people had with him had not been as easy. I couldn't believe my luck.

During one of my first visits to the Marian Boys' Boxing Club I stood with the back of my head against the wall, trying to make myself as inconspicuous as possible. The back of my head touched a row of eight electrical switches and one of the lads thought it would be great fun to swing a punch bag in my direction. I moved swiftly to get out of the way of the bag and in the process smashed my head into the switches. I broke every one of those switches with my head. The result was that I had a very sore head and an indent on my skull to correspond with every switch that was on that wall. Nevertheless, I was not given any sympathy. Instead, I was asked why I was smashing the place up on my very first night! I had great difficulty in explaining the situation. I always felt that they hadn't fully believed me but of course, as I was the new kid on the block and the others weren't too helpful in coming to my aid, this didn't surprise me.

As I've already mentioned, this club didn't conduct boxing in a very professional way. It was more of a youth club than an organised boxing club. Some nights there would be people to give the training and supervise the proceedings and on other nights there wouldn't be anyone – it was the luck of the draw as to what was to happen on the night. Of course, on the nights that the trainers hadn't turned up, the lads would run riot and have a good old mess around. On these nights the whole experience would be even more daunting as the lads would make sure that they got people like me into the ring to demonstrate how good their skills in boxing were. After my very first night at the club I was absolutely certain that boxing wasn't for me. The only thing I had learnt was that if you get in the ring somebody is going to hit you – and hit you bloody hard. At this point there had been nothing about teaching you how not to be hit and how to hit without dropping your guard. So, my experience from the first night at boxing was a very, very rude awakening to say the least.

That night in the boxing club in Wicklow town I left the club with my head in a state. My main problem was how I could tell my foster father that I didn't want to do any-more of this boxing. I just couldn't find any way of putting it across to him that I was a coward, and that I wasn't wanting to do it. I just couldn't tell him so I had to put all my fears to the back of my mind and head back in to the next week's training. Occasionally, they would have a trainer there and I was lucky this night as the trainer was Frank Kerr. He was from Dublin and he had actually boxed in the Golden Glove compe-tition in America for the Irish team back in 1933. In those days they used to pay the trainers 30 shillings an hour – good money in the Fifties – as nobody ever helped out the youngsters in amateur sport for nothing. Whatever the motivation, I greatly appreciated the help that Mr Kerr gave me and soon I was a familiar face at the Marian Club.

At least on the nights when the trainer was there I didn't get a hammering but I knew that I would have to come up with a strategy to survive the occasions when the trainer was absent again. I started thinking, strangely enough, of my experiences with the goats on the hills, because no matter how much I chased them and ran after them they always out ran me and I just ended up exhausted. So that's what I tried to do. Copying the goats' tactics, I got into the ring and, no matter who the fight was with, I didn't set about having World War Three with him but tried to keep out of the way instead. I learned to weave, run and skip (and never in a straight line) as hard and as fast as I could. I didn't care what I did and how I looked as long as I kept away from being clobbered. As things progressed I got a little bit better at avoiding punches and, of course, the art of boxing is all about managing to hit without being hit.

Shortly after, a new boxing club started up at Barndarrig and I was informed that a lad there by the name of Sean Roach was gunning for me because of my connections with the Wicklow club. The lad would have been just a bit older, but a lot heavier than I was. Local gossip left me in no doubt that when they got the two of us in the one ring then my goose would be cooked. This was a very worrying time for me as I used to go around in fear of being dragged into the ring at Barndarrig and being made to fight him. Apart from the fear of a beating, I was also frightened that I would look very silly at the end of the fight. You see, if I had been boxing somebody from far away I wouldn't have felt so bad about it but somebody from a few miles away was a different cup of tea. Looking back on it now it is funny how people can build up such a local rivalry between two young lads to the point where it could affect your sleep because of the hype and you always forget that the other lad probably isn't feeling much better.

Still, if anyone mentioned the name Roach to me I would come over in a cold sweat. Everyone seemed well aware of this lad's talent. I believed what they were saying and was not pleased – to say the least – that they were having me over to spar with this guy. I was going to be pulverised for their pleasure. Of course, the lads and the blokes around the area took great pleasure in winding me up as they would with a young lad in those days. This banter went on for months so when the postman, old Mick Hetherington (who had actually started the club in Barndarrig) told me that it had been arranged that I was to meet Roach in their church hall for us to commence battle with all of our local supporters mingling around, I can tell you that if I say that I was not over-confident I wouldn't have been underestimating things. I couldn't sleep because of the fear of meeting this great ferocious lad.

The dreadful night arrived and I had to cycle over to Barndarrig to face my fears. They put the gloves first on Roach and then they came to me and by this time I had a job to stop shivering with fear. When the bell struck to start round one I soon discovered that Roach was indeed a very game lad who wasn't taking prisoners. It was do or die. The training that I had had recently at the Wicklow club kicked in and I found that I had learnt more than I had realised. I met Roach's charge with a perfectly timed, well-executed left hook and to my amazement all of the lad's teeth dropped out of his mouth and on to the canvas. They had sheared right off at gum level. You see, it was not just my punch that did this damage, as the poor guy had pyorrhoea of the gums. This contributed to a very quick conclusion to the fight and I'm glad to say I was never asked back to prove who was the greatest!

Instead of him having stripped me of my pride and respect, the crowd actually lifted me head and shoulders over the whole area because I had succeeded in something that was commonly believed to be an impossibility. I would meet some of the locals a long time after the fight and they would still be going on about what a great performance I had put on in Barndarrig. They confessed that I was much better than they could have imagined. 'Good man, Donald,' they would say 'you did a great job. You'll be world champion; you'll be the fear of Ireland.' Others said 'Donald, bejesus you were great the other night, you're an absolute topper.' Little did they know that I hadn't slept for a month due to the fear of my impending fight. It just goes to show how life can turn. Mick Hetherington, the local postman, was as proud as punch that I had done so well. While I was over at his club, I went into the gym to show some of his lads what life was all about in boxing. I would have thought that Mick might have had his tail between his legs but no, he appeared to be was as proud of me as if I had of been one of his own lads.

Through that fight I built a reputation that was a thousand times better than what I was in reality. For the locals, it was soon going around that I was the hottest thing since Rocky Marciano! I suppose one way of summing up my local fame would be that 'a one eyed man is a king in a blind man's world'. This is where the confidence started that was to last a long time, as I went on to fight for thirty-three years as an amateur boxer. I boxed at five different weights and won the British Territorial Army championships at three different weights. Who would have believed it from that little wretch that used to run across the rocks with the goats in the Wicklow hills? Although I had more confidence as a result of my success, I was still struggling with myself. I am sure that I didn't achieve as much in the boxing world as I could or should have done due to my lack of self-esteem and faith in my own ability. Still, it was great to find something I was good at.

I remember my first 'proper' competitive boxing bout very well. It was near the Delahunt in Wicklow. There was a dance hall there behind the forge and of course, because of the badly organized club that I was with, I wouldn't have been too well trained and I didn't really know what to do. I was soon to discover just how tough and ferocious the world of competitive boxing could be. Some people had lent me some white boxing shorts and a white vest and when I finished that bout both my shorts and my vest were bright red with blood. My opponent was from Wexford, he was a young lad by the name of Moor. The fight wasn't that savage but he managed to hit me a couple times straight on the nose. I seemed to bleed easily as I had some pretty horrific nose bleeds over the years. I suppose that during my boxing career I probably lost enough blood to keep a hospital in stock for a week!

Another fight in particular stands out in my mind. It was when I was matched with a lad from the Belvedere Boxing Club in Dublin. The lad I was matched against didn't turn up and they were short of fights. They weren't too fussy about the age or the correct weight at this time – unlike today under the ABA rules. If you looked anything like near enough the right stature then you were matched with whomever they decided to put you with. The lad they eventually decided to put me against was quite a bit bigger than me and he certainly had been around the ring a few times more than I could have dreamt about so he was quite a capable kid as I was to find out. He gave me a right good pasting when we got in the ring. Oddly enough against all of the obstacles that I had to face, for some unknown reason I ploughed through and kept on going. I obviously was getting better at it, though I didn't realise it.

It is odd that I continued with the boxing even though at times I had grave misgivings about it. It was not through choice that I kept going but more out of fear and me not wanting the fear to show. It was also the fear of letting down my foster father and disgracing him, added to the fear of his big leather belt across my backside. These were the sorts of things that had to be weighed up. The decision that I made was that it would be worse for me to pack in the boxing and take what might come (depending on whether my foster father had been on beer or not). I vowed to do my best to carry on the boxing as I figured that in recompense for getting a hiding in the ring, I might be getting some sort of recognition for it. There wouldn't be a lot of recognition for not doing it. Maybe when someone has been belittled and put down all his life, he will go to great lengths to achieve something. If there is a chance of him getting some recognition for doing something that is not the norm for all the other lads in the area, it would be worth it. After my first fight it was amazing the amount of people who took an interest in how I was actually doing in the boxing world. A lot of people were starting to give me the respect that I never thought possible. In the boxing ring I suppose I was as tough as it was possible for somebody in my situation to be. This was something, I thought, that I could never have possibly achieved in any other way, and whilst I was young I still had a few more contests in the area.

Nothing, however, ran smoothly in my life and more complications were to come in my direction. One night, one of the lads asked me if I knew that there was a cup of tea and a bun available for a penny at the end of the training session – and of course I believed him. I was assured that the bun was very good and large for a penny. This sounded good to me on a freezing wet winter's night when I would have had a six mile bike ride to face on my way back. The next night I trooped in behind the rest of them to have this cup of tea but things weren't as simple as that. This is when I found out that this was a Roman Catholic boxing club. It was run by a priest by the name of Father Hans. When I got in to the room everybody had to sit down in the chairs that were laid out in rows and start praying. Well, being Church of Ireland, I didn't know anything about rosary beads and stuff like that and I was like a fish out of water. I was wishing for the ground to open up and swallow me – anything to take me out of this awkward situation. Needless to say, the next night that I went, I didn't go for a cup of tea and a bun. These events meant that I had to tell my foster father that there was a priest involved in the boxing club. He didn't stop me going to the club altogether as I thought he would have, but he did give me a very severe warning. He said to me, 'You make sure you don't call him Father.' and added 'He isn't your father. You can call him sir, but don't call him Father'. I understood what my foster father was telling me but when you face this sort situation in reality, it's a very different matter and I suffered a very, very awkward moment the very next night. The priest came up to me and asked why I hadn't gone in to prayers the night before. I started fumbling, stammering and looking down at my feet as I just didn't know what to say. I didn't know what to call him – sir or Father. I thought it was very odd for me to be calling him sir when nobody else was calling him that, so I closed my eyes and called him Father. I wished with all my heart that I could get away but eventually I managed to get a few words of explanation out. 'Well Father, I'm not a Roman Catholic.' 'Oh,' he said, with some surprise 'you're not,' and then he asked 'What are you?' I swallowed hard and said 'I'm Church of Ireland.' He looked closely at me and asked, 'and what prayers do you say then?' 'I say Our Father, I say the Creed, like everybody does, and I pray for everybody to be kept safe.' 'No,' he said 'no, you don't say the Creed, or Our Father "like everybody",' he said 'because it's only you and I, who are Christians, who say the Creed and Our Father.' Well I can tell you I was quite flabbergasted by this. Obviously in the climate that I was raised in, you always had a lot of suspicion and mistrust when it came to anyone else's religion. You would be fearful of what might happen because of some of the stories you would hear. The tales told locally about religion rivalled those told about ghosts. For example, I had heard that nuns wore long skirts so they could pinch children, hide them under their skirts and take them off to the monastery. So I kept well clear of the nuns as a child. We always heard that the priests would want to convert us and with all of this running through our minds we were often confused to say the least.

This experience left me reluctant to go to the boxing club so I left and with that I'm afraid my boxing training came to an end for a while. I also had to forego that lovely bun and that cup of tea. I didn't get involved with prayers or other religious aspects of life and as that was part of the deal at St Marian's, I had to leave. God knows, I would have loved to be able to enjoy that bun but it wasn't to be.

During this period some of the old boys loved to see the young lads scrapping and would engineer impromptu bouts with the greatest of pleasure. There was one old guy by the name of Bradshaw who kept the forge in Dunganstown and used to work for the council filling the potholes. It is said that in his younger days he used to give the kids sweets for whoever won the scrap so it encouraged kids to fight, as a bag of sweets was something to really aim for. There wouldn't be too many kids from poor backgrounds that would have the opportunity to get sweets very often, so they jumped at the opportunity. The kids would often just pretend to fight. One would forfeit the fight so that the other could win the fight and get the bag of sweets – but then, of course, when they got up the road they would share the sweets between them. I believe that this went on for quite some time without him ever realising that they were having him on.

Mr Bradshaw was one of the most miserable old goats you could ever come across. I met him when was I was tidying our pathway up to the schoolhouse, as he used to go across our pathway with buckets of water to fill a tub for his cattle. For some unknown reason one day he took the view that I was trying to make his journey awkward and he ran out after me. I dropped the old shovel I was holding and ran like crazy. When I looked behind me down the road I could see him with the shovel desperately trying to catch up with me.

My success in the ring and my increased self-confidence still didn't make me forget the thoughts that haunted me at night or when I was on my own. My mind would wonder back to my adoption and the fostering business as this was as much a part of my life as the boxing. People often asked if I was adopted or fostered. A lot of people in Ireland were in the same boat I as was with regard to their legal situation. I was adopted as far as my foster family were concerned, though, as I've said, there were no legal adoptions in Southern Ireland until after 1952. Nevertheless, it was still a phrase used on a regular basis to me. I was labelled on many occasions as a bastard, an adoptee or foster child. I always felt fear when I heard these words as they would cut me so deeply. I grew up feeling such shame and when somebody used these words against me it would be like chucking a bucket of cold water over me. I would just shudder. Why did I did feel ashamed, I often wonder? What could I have done about it? I had no part to play in being a bastard, being adopted or being fostered. I was just a victim of the situation like many thousands of children in Ireland at that time.

Chapter 12

Growing up too soon

I left school at the age of 13 unable to read or write, and became as good as a slave to farmers who would pay me what they liked, when they liked. I had a series of casual jobs with farmers before I started doing farm work on a permanent basis. At 15 I worked for a farmer seven days a week from seven in the morning until late at night and basically I was working for my food and a roof over my head – but more of that life later. There was no money left over from my wages to buy any of the things that a normal teenager would want. All the money that I earned up until my late teens – whether from my farm work or from one of my enterprises such as the turkeys I kept, or things I would grow – went to buy food for the whole of the family rather than just for me. For most of the time my money appeared to be supporting the whole family including my foster aunts.

One thing that I was desperate to buy with

the money I earned was a pair of long trousers. Believe it or not, I spent the first couple of years of my 'adult' working life in children's short trousers. As soon as I left school, the trousers gave me a particular problem when the time for my confirmation was announced. Of course, this is an important occasion in the Church of Ireland as it marks the passage from childhood to adulthood but I really didn't want to go through with it as I felt I had nothing suitable to wear. Short trousers just wouldn't do in my eyes.

Daisy stepped in and went to see Reverend Burke to tell him that if he wanted me to be confirmed then the poor box would have to give us some funds to kit me out. The poor fund of the parish – money that came from people's wills that was intended to help poor Church of Ireland people and their families – had always been there but the only time that we had ever received any funds from it was when Molly got confirmed. I'm not sure why this was but the responsibility for distribution of the funds lay with the clergyman of the parish. It appeared however that in Dunganstown none of the vicars that passed through the parish during the time I was growing up ever thought that it was necessary to give any of the fund to the parish's local starving families.

Back to Daisy's efforts. As smart as Reverend Burke was, he hadn't reckoned on Miss Daisy Reynolds in full flight. Normally a very shrewd character and quiet in her approach, she was very difficult to rattle, but believe me when she went over the line of balanced, shrewd, intelligent thinking she was something else! Reverend Burke had the fright of his life when she told him off. She said in no uncertain terms that if it were important to him to confirm me then he would have to go to his poor box and get the money out to buy me the clothes that were necessary for this occasion. So, to my surprise, Daisy told me that Reverend Burke had agreed to buy me a new suit of clothes for my confirmation. I had to go to the McDonald's shop in Wicklow, a gent's outfitters shop owned by a brother of Willie McDonald of the castle. She had arranged, to poor old Burke's horror, that he would have to take us all in and get us all rigged out for the event and this included my foster brother as well!

On arriving in the shop the old gentleman in charge led me to where he would be fitting me out for this new suit. He stopped to fetch the clothes from off of the rack and I looked in dismay as he was laying them out.

'This can't be for me, because they are short trousers.'

He looked at me with disdain and replied 'This is what has been arranged for you. I am sorry, this is what you are having.' Well I couldn't believe it as I was now well past my fourteenth birthday. Reverend Burke, for whatever reason, had arranged for me to continue wearing short trousers. My sheer excitement and happiness at finally getting some new clothes disappeared in a split second and all my old fears and frustrations returned. I had already been working full time for 12 months and having to go about in short trousers while trying to get work and being in work was not easy. I was always afraid that people would think that I was having them on about my age. I knew that they probably would not have told that me that I wasn't suitably dressed for their employment – they would simply not want me near the place. I thought about what a miserable bastard the vicar was as I realised that, for the sake of saving a couple of bob, he had denied me the chance to get regular employment rather than the odd jobs I had to take.

Despite my lack of long trousers, Confirmation day arrived. Because of the importance of the event, there were more clergymen in the parish than normal and also the bishop attended, with the result that the church was quite full. One of the visiting clergymen was quite a well-set person and when he walked, his cassock made him look as if he was waddling from side to side like a big, fat penguin. I have to say that this made the ceremony a nightmare for me because I just could not stop laughing. I was getting kicked and dug in the ribs for continually laughing and being a nuisance to the whole show. I was told in no uncertain terms that I was a disgrace to the solemn ceremony.

I didn't forget my desire for long trousers, especially when the parish Christmas party came around, I tried to earn a bit extra one year so that I could get those trousers. Coming up to Christmas I had heard that Fleming's were buying holly at the Dublin market so I launched myself into the holly business. I set about, six weeks before Christmas, to collect some of the holly that was abundant in our area. I was told that it was a shilling a bunch and I collected it far and wide. It often meant going on to some of the local farmers' land to get this holly. It never even crossed my mind that I might be trespassing – as far as I was concerned there was no boundaries. One or two people did not approve. Mrs Walker, for instance, gave me a dreadful dressing down for going on her land and taking the holly off her trees. She didn't change my mind though. I thought it wasn't really a big deal because the holly would have stayed there if I hadn't taken it. All I wanted to do was buy myself a pair of trousers. While she told me off, I was thinking to myself, 'If you were doing your job right I wouldn't need to resort to this' as I had become increasingly angry about how the guardians at the orphanage had neglected their duties. Despite her warnings, I just carried on as I was.

I had gone miles collecting the holly and had a huge stack of the prickly stuff at the bottom of the old schoolhouse garden, just behind the old stone wall. I was in a state of high excitement when the Fleming's van turned up to collect it. I thought that I would have a big pile of money coming my way for my efforts. I got the shock of my life because there had been a misunderstanding about the bundles that I was told I could sell for a shilling. By bundles they had meant stacks the size of hay bundles. My poor pile of holly looked very small indeed and at the end of the day I only got a few quid for the whole effort. My new long trousers were only that pipe dream once more and yet again at the parish Christmas party I was dressed in rags. I started to wonder if I would ever achieve my ambition of looking like a young man.

Without those trousers I just knew that the parish's children's Christmas party would be a nightmare – and I was right. I was in the loo and one of the lads from the other school at Red Cross was there also. He was making a great fuss about how difficult it was to have a wee when wearing long trousers as he had got brand new cord trousers on. He was winding me up by pretending that it was awkward to get the fly open and done up again. He was about two years younger than me so I felt doubly embarrassed that I was still in short trousers – and short trousers that were merely rags. He turned to me and said 'you're all right because you can pull the leg of your trousers up and get on with it, where as I've got to struggle with getting this fly open'. There I was in short trousers being goaded by a lad two years younger than me and all I wanted was the long trousers. Yet again, I felt inferior and the celebration was ruined for me.

I suspected that my short trousers did not help my employment prospects and one incident that proved this was when I went to work for the new man that had taken over old Sam Cole's shop in Kilbouyed. His name was Mr Gaynor and he used it to take his turf lorry around to the farmers along with coal and logs. He also used to have a regular run from Arklow Pottery to Dublin to take the pottery to the wholesalers for distributing around their outlets. I worked with them for a week but at the end of the week he said to me that I was too small for the job and that I would have to come back and see him in about three months. Well I can tell you that I was extremely upset with that particular news because I had been having a good ride around on the lorry, going to places that I had never seen before.

Several people advised me to do something different other than casual farm work but it seemed impossible to me to make the leap to steady, satisfying employment. There was an old forge in Kilcandra where an old guy worked who was almost a hundred. I used to spend a bit of time talking to him and I was amazed with all the stuff that he had and all the different types of tools. He said many times to me, 'You should look at taking something like this up instead of allowing yourself to be used as a donkey, there is no future in what you are doing young lad. Try and get on to something different.' Well, he was a wise and lovely chap.

A farmer nearby approached me to tell me that he wanted me to start with him if I wished. He was new in the area, from Meath and he was a cattle dealer. His name was Mr Riley and he had quite a few sons. I didn't take too much notice of what he said as I had some casual work at the time but he was true to his word. When my job was over he was passing by and he asked 'Can you start next Monday?' and of course, that's what I did. I got on well with him and his sons; there was a set of twins Oliver and Norbert and he also had a son or two in England at the time.

I was paid three pounds a week, and my duties were milking the cows, feeding the animals, sometimes helping with new stock that was bought from other farmers who dealt in livestock, chopping timber up for logs and sawing down trees. I would then have to go and deliver the timber logs to customers in the nearby towns with one of his five sons. I got on well with this farmer but I was soon to find out that the more I was able to do, the more I had to do. I often had to plough the fields with two horses. Some of these fields were very rocky and when the plough hit one of these rocks, the plough would virtually somersault taking me with it, as I was not much taller than the plough handles at the time. I had to load the horse and cart with large timbers that were to be sawn up in the yard. I would have to travel down the steep hills with the heavy loads and the harness often snapped and then the cart and load would tip backwards. The harness that was being used had long since passed its sell-by date. Also, I would have to load the horse cart with farm dung to top-dress the fields. A day's work pro- gressively became longer and longer and it was a seven-day a week job with no days off. I often accompanied the cattle wagon to fetch animals that had been bought in other parts of the country and would not get back till late at night. I would then have to head home on my clapped out pushbike. This was never a pleasant journey after a day's work, particularly in the winter when the weather was bad and the nights were black and menacing out in the countryside. I used to have to cycle past a big country estate that had seen better days. I had heard stories that a previous owner used to stand at the rear gates with his head under his arm. I was cycling one night and as I was approaching this gateway I got a puncture in my rear wheel. I have to say that I did not make any attempt to sort out the puncture whatsoever. My imagination took over, my courage failed me and I just got off the bike and ran as fast as my legs would take me.

Although the hours were always long, sometimes they were made even longer by extra jobs that the farmer would come up with. One winter's night after finishing all the farm jobs, the farmer approached me at about five o'clock in pitch black and told me that I had to go to the Ashford sales yard to bring back a herd of sheep that consisted of about four hundred sheep. I only had a push-bike without a light and had no sheepdog or any other help whatsoever. As if this wasn't bad enough, I knew that the sales yard was about twelve miles away. When I got there, the people at the sales yard asked, 'Where's the rest of the gang to help you take them back? You will need them.' I replied 'You must be joking', at which they advised me that, 'an army wouldn't take this lot back tonight. It will be impossible to get them across the main Wexford and Dublin road never mind the laneways.' I didn't budge. The man in charge looked me straight in the eye and said 'Young fellow, you must be mad. As soon as the sheep see a car light coming at them they will scatter all over the place.' Despite my size and age I'd been doing farm work for some years by this time so I told them that I was under no illusions as how difficult it was going to be but that I had no choice; I had been told that I had to get them all back.

They could see that I was determined and said 'Okay young fellow, if that's what you think you have to do but we are telling you now that nobody in their right mind could expect a kid like you to do it on your own.' I knew that the men were telling me the truth and were very concerned for me and I found out on the way back just how right they were. Despite the obvious difficulties, I got back about four in the morning without having even one sheep lost. The farmer told me off when I arrived back 'What in God's name has taken you so long to get back?' he yelled, 'For Jesus' sake I could have been to Belfast and back in that time!' His wife said nothing but brought me out a very welcome cup of tea. The week after I looked at my pay and noticed he had not given me any extra at all for fetching his bloody sheep. I approached him and told him that there was nothing extra for working through the night with the sheep. His only response was to say 'For Jesus' sake, didn't you get a cup of tea?' and there was no money or other reward forthcoming. To be fair to him he did pay me my three pounds every week without fail and this, as I was to find out later when I worked for other farmers, wasn't always the case – some of them would only pay when it suited them.

I left Riley's when I was told that Tom Earls (who played in Jim Burn's Band) had to go to work for Colonel Clark so he was leaving Callaghan's farm. I managed to get taken on by the Callaghan brothers – twin brothers who were very big lads and could be quite an imposing sight. When I first started there it was a seven-day a week job that included milking cows, harvesting crops, feeding and cleaning out animals and ploughing with horses. Many of the jobs were really hard for a lad of my size. For example, when I was working on the harvest I would put a rope around the butt of the cock of hay and use a ratchet handle to drag it up onto the bogie. When the cock of hay was over the central point of the bogie the weight of the cock would weigh it down and it would then trigger a mechanism that would secure the cart in a lock-down position. The bogie had large wide metal wheels to save it from sinking into the ground; you could only use this in dry weather because if you used it in the wet weather it would sink down to the axle. You would have to take the hay to the haggert and throw it up onto a rick of hay in the hay shed. This was almost impossible work for a young lad but I suppose that all of my previous experiences were coming into play, as it didn't seem to matter the difficulties in doing the different types of jobs, I just got on with it.

When I started for Callaghan's I was again paid three pounds a week plus my food and they treated me as well as any person. They gave me the run of the house and treated me no different to any family member when it came to being seated at their table to eat. This certainly was not always the case with other farmers and their labourers. In many cases farm workers wouldn't be allowed to eat in the house but had to eat in a corner in an outhouse. I can only say that they treated me no different than if had I been a part of their family.

This was great but then they came up with the idea that I would be better moving in and I was installed in the spare bedroom. My foster father was dead against me living in on the job but he never said why. Make no mistake, he dearly loved me around the place and me in his own way but I couldn't guess the reasons for his objections.

I knew that the new arrangements meant that my day would not commence at eight in the morning and finish at six in the evening but it would be like being in the army where you would be on call twenty-four hours a day. When I first started there both John and Henry would help me but it seemed to me that as time went by they were more away from the farm than they were on it and the burden of most of the work would fall on me. When John got married this situation became even worse, as Henry seemed to have lost the plot altogether. Before John's wedding, the two had been inseparable and went drinking together (too much for their own good sometimes) and dancing was often the order of the day but, left to his own devices, Henry became more interested than ever in the dance halls and the pubs and that meant that my day and my week never ended. I was virtually doing everything on my own, and instead of being paid weekly I was paid whenever it suited Henry.

As hard as I had to work, from time to time I did get a laugh. I had to drive a little International tractor that was like driving an MG Saloon as it had a good handful of gears. Poor old John Callaghan found this out to his cost when he was taking the piss out of me one winter day. 'Haven't you got that yoke going yet?' he asked me as I tinkered with the machine. I replied rather reluctantly that I couldn't get it to start and big John immediately took matters into his own hands and climbed aboard the tractor. He was very determined to show me how to do it properly, shouting as he climbed up 'Silly young pup'. Try as he may, however, he could not get even a puff of smoke out of it. He was annoyed with finding himself in this embarrassing situation and he called out for his brother Henry to give him a push. Henry and I were setting ourselves to be in the best position to push this tractor and as we were about to take off I spotted that the gear lever was engaged in a very fast gear. I had previously experienced this tractor's full capability on many hair-raising occasions but I don't think that either John or Henry had ever had known its full capability. I did try to tell John that his choice of gear was not good but he would have none of it. He persisted in believing that he had made the best choice in this matter and we could do no more than push him as requested. By now he was really wound up with the situation, so Henry and I were pushing like hell. Suddenly the tractor burst into full flight leaving Henry and me face down in shit whilst John was hanging on for dear life as he smashed through two gates in the cow lane. For good measure, John had also lost his hat. When he got back after leaving the tractor at the bottom of the lane he was still shaking but, needless to say, made no comment about his choice of gears. I didn't mention it either as it all happened so quickly – we were all too dumbstruck by John's lightning start. After this, in the event of a tractor not starting, I noticed that it would be me who would have to mount the beast!

My foster brother Sean sometimes used to drift down to see me at work, to see if I had any money that he could have. I would always give him something to eat. At that time the farm was overrun by rats. As we had a double-barrel shotgun, Sean and I came up with the idea of putting corn on an old wooden pig trough and we would lean out of a bedroom window with the shotgun on the window ledge. We would take turns in switching the yard light on and then open fire in the direction of the rats that had gathered around the corn. Each time we would make an inspection of where the rats had been feeding and always found the pig trough riddled with pellets but to our horror we never found any dead rats in the area. We would really have expected a few dozen at a time, but days later I would notice wounded rats all over the place, limping around. To say rats are tough is an under statement!

After our shooting exploits one evening I was putting the shotgun away when I met John in the hallway where the gun was kept. On seeing the shotgun John completely froze. He reacted in such a way that you would have thought that somebody had hit him on the head with a hammer. When Henry came in and saw what the situation was he said 'Oh my God, put the gun away. You must never let John see you with the gun.' He explained to me what had happened to make his brother react to guns in this way. Apparently, John had been sitting on the mudguard of Joe Heavener's tractor and Joe's son Digby (who was a terrible prankster) was out shooting rabbits with his rifle. He spotted John sitting on the mudguard and took careful aim at his hat putting a hole right through the upper part of his hat. From that day John could never stand to be near anybody carrying a firearm and he would just freak out.

Sometimes I would go down to see Paddy Doyle (even though Paddy was the man who used to disgust me by taking his false teeth out when I was a little lad in Dunganstown). Paddy would not normally have been considered a likely person to put up with a sixteen-year-old, as he was a most serious type of man with a very short fuse. To me, however, he was a great friend and I found him very informative. He was more than capable of debating any topic, even with his self-opinionated views on all subjects and he would almost go into orbit in his commanding way.

Paddy was one of those people who could put the fear of God into you and he wasn't everyone's cup of tea as he was a prophet of what was to become of us. For example, he believed that motor cars would become obsolete and that we would all be getting around in spaceships or he would be predicting another great war; a war that would be intense and destructive to structures and human beings alike. My daughters were to meet Paddy many years later and were hypnotized by his outbursts but by then he was in his eighties. I spent many a long night listening to him and all of his doom and gloom and watched his television. I loved every minute of it. He had views on almost every subject and I never tired of listening to him. He would tell me of his exploits – how some poachers who were after his rabbits laid in wait for him and hit him over the head with an iron bar. He would be raving on and insisting that 'The bloody bastards nearly killed me!' He was also a wonderful piano accordionist and on a summer's evening you could hear him for miles and he could also entertain you with his very convincing bird impressions. Apart from the musical entertainment he had plenty of hobbies. He renovated old railway carriages to a very high standard – all self-taught – and he kept loads of beehives so that his main diet was bread and honey. He accused one of the local farmers of destroying his bees with crop spraying. As odd as Paddy may have been taken, he may have had a point when it comes to this pollution as there is now a lot more than bees being destroyed. The whole natural world is in danger.

With Paddy you either liked him or disliked him but say what you like about him he was a very talented man. You also had to give Paddy credit for the way he had lived his life. His wife left him with six children, which he raised himself, unaided. He ruled the household with a rod of iron and I think that his sons and daughters all emigrated to England but his sons never returned and I understand that only one of his daughters would visit him.

Another diversion that I had from the daily grind was that sometimes I would meet up with my foster father to go and watch a hurling match in Ashford or Rathnew. He loved to go to the matches with me and in his own little way he had become very proud of me. If he had any money in his pocket or if I had any in mine, which was not very often, he would not be able to pass a pub without going into it. I hated this. I would be so frustrated hanging about in the pub because the only thing I wanted to do was to get to the match. I suppose that is one reason why to this day I have very little interest in pubs. Of course, when the match was over work would beckon again. I would have to go back to Callaghan's to milk the cows and feed and bed down all of the animals. Looking back now I cannot understand why this weekend work was never shared though at the time I never grumbled. It didn't occur to me that it might be unfair that I never had a day off during the twelve months of the year. Whilst I was at Callaghan's I always had good food even if I had to work around the clock for it so I do not want to give the impression that John and Henry Callaghan were bad people. That was definitely not the case but in the case of paying me and giving me time off this was where they fell short.

Another character in my life while I was working at Callaghan's farm was an old lady called Miss White who was an ex-music teacher and lived with the Callaghan brothers. Apparently the loss of her own two brothers who had been killed in the first World War and also the loss of her two sons severely affected the balance of her mind. It was said that her daughter was affected in the same way by looking after her mother. Miss White was very unpredictable and would often get up in the middle of the night to play her piano. This could be very annoying when you were trying to sleep and therefore it was decided that two of the outer houses would be done up for her so she could do more of her own thing without disturbing the household. One of her little 'rooms', as she referred to them, was Ivy Lodge and the other was

226

called Violet Lodge.

One night I was awoken by a fuss being made by Miss White, who told me that Violet Lodge was on fire. I told her to go back to bed but she came rapping on the windows telling me the same tale. By this time I suppose I had woken up a bit more and thought that maybe I should take her more seriously. When I looked out of the window I could see that she was telling me the truth – the flames were already strong and frightening. I had to do something but it was pointless to go to the pump in the yard as that had dried up during the long dry summer of that year – 1958. I decided I would get some old wheat sacks and soak them in the brook down the road. I only had a shirt on and I was in my bare feet running to the brook to soak the sacks in the water. When I got back I dragged all of the burning furniture from the room into the yard but as fast as I was throwing it out she was carrying it all back in again. It was a nightmare. I managed to get the fire out and then to calm her down but her main concern was that all of her cats were all right. We discovered the cause of the fire later. Because we wouldn't give her the paraffin that she had wanted earlier in the day (we knew it wouldn't be safe with her) she had looked around and found some diesel from somewhere and, in an action typical of her confused behaviour, had put this in a glass paraffin lamp. The lamp had, of course, exploded, setting fire to everything. Her eccentricity knew no bounds but was usually less harmful than these actions. For example, it wouldn't matter what furniture you gave her she would never be satisfied with its style and she continually attempted to make her own alterations. She would find a saw and saw lumps off every chair or table until she was happy with it.

I enjoyed my trips out with my foster father, visits to Paddy Doyle and so on and even Miss White's antics added excitement to my life, but most of it was made up of sheer hard work. The ploughing on this farm was particularly difficult because of the soil. You would be weighed down with the sticky soil. When I was ploughing with the horses and going up and down the furrow I would have a couple of stone in weight of mud stuck to me, which was very tiring as the day wore on. It would drain the muscles in your legs so we would try to find the driest time in spring and take full advantage of any dry spell that came our way in terms in preparing the ground for sowing. This often meant that when they got the old Fordson tractor out it would mean working very late (and in some cases all night) to take the advantage of the dry weather. Things were always worse in winter, of course, and when you were taking the cows in and out for milking, the gateways to the fields you would often go down to your armpits in shit and it would be a frequent experience to lose your Wellingtons! It wasn't just during harvest or ploughing times that we had to work through the night either. When the sow was giving birth to her litter or when the cows were calving you would have to attend to them whatever time of day or night it was. These occasions were always very highly charged, as you would never know until after the event was over if everything was going to be okay or not and if things were to go bad I would feel responsible for any loss which could have occurred to any of the livestock. It would always hit me very hard if any animals died.

Although I was growing up fast and working so hard and long that, by rights, I should have been asleep the moment my head hit the pillow, I often used to lay awake during the long winter nights. I would still be wondering about where had I originated from and who were my real parents. The mystery lady who screamed for me to be given back to her would always enter my thoughts at night too as I settled down to sleep. I had reached young adulthood without finding any answers to the questions that had always tormented me. I dreamed of finding the answers and understanding why my life was as it was.

Chapter 13

Holy Men

As you will know by now, I hold the Church of Ireland and its people partially responsible for many of the problems that befell me in my younger days and also for some of the effects that are still giving me a hard time even now in my later years. However, as with everything in this life, the people of the Church of Ireland were certainly not universally bad. I was never too far from the Church in my boyhood – it held all sorts of opportunities for me socially and also as a source of work – as in those days the church took central stage in every village's life. The men (and in those days they were invariably men as women priests were as yet unheard of) who preached in the parish church or played some other part in my life were a diverse mix – some good, some bad.

The first clergyman that I came into contact with was Reverend Foster, who was in the parish for over twenty years and was a proper gentleman. He was certainly a God-fearing man who tried to do his best by every one of his parishioners and no one would have said a bad word against him. Indeed, he was thought well of by all of his neighbours of different religions. What puzzles me about Reverend Foster is that this very caring man was, in fact, the man who helped to arrange my adoption. He must have known that my going to this family was not serving my best interests. He would have known only too well of the extreme conditions of poverty that I was going to be subjected to. He would also have known that there was a parish poor fund to assist poor families just like the family that I was part of after I was fostered. However, he never did anything about it and to me this just goes to show how blind people can be. They can pretend to themselves and to the outside world that every thing is great, even though they know it is not. As usual in the Church of Ireland it is about keeping up appearances. Apart from this aspect, you could not have met a nicer person than Reverend Foster and we all felt sad when he left us for his new parish in Ashford.

There was a silver lining to this cloud, however, as when the old vicar was moving out of the rectory at Dunganstown our foster father received a little bit of cash for helping them move. This was particularly welcome at this time because as a family we were, yet again, struggling financially. Partly this was due to the lack of continuity in my foster father's work. In the early fifties the combine harvester was starting to come in and the thrashing machines were starting to become redundant. As he was sometimes employed as a farm labourer using the thrashing machines, this was to have an adverse effect on my foster father's employment during that summer and we needed every penny that we could lay our hands on.

When we helped the vicar and his family to move there was cartload after cartload of empty bottles. We took these loads of bottles from their cellars down to a big hole in one of the fields to dump them. These empty bottles were obviously useless, but we also removed loads of things from the house that we thought were absolutely marvellous. There were lots of old kid's toys including my favourite, spud guns. We sieved through the junk to find the things we liked and had them for ourselves. It was amazing to us the amount of good stuff that they were dumping. There were kitchen items such as plates, cups and mugs and every kind of utensil and there were even a few oil paintings. There were all sorts of mechanical things like prams, bikes and scrap of bikes and I made sure I had these things for myself and set to work as soon as we had finished the move to put these things to good use. I made carts with wheels so that I would be able to carry firewood easily. Out of all the bits of old bikes I managed to make a bike of sorts though it was a bit of a bodged job. The crank was missing and I had to hammer lead in to the axle as a bearing and to take some of the slack out of the gap. This meant that when the lead wore down I had a very wonky pedalling motion. When I refer to a clapped out bike that I rode to get me to various jobs – this was the bike. We kids played with the discarded tyres. We used to send the old car tyres down the big hill that led to the old church and the old castle. The cars coming up would be dodging the tyres that were coming down and, of course, the drivers would not be in the least bit amused by this prank but we thought it great fun as we watched and giggled. The Reverend Foster's move out of the parish had given our family plenty of opportunities – money for my foster father, plenty of salvaged goods and some fun for us kids.

Mr Foster was later to become Canon for the parish of Nun's Cross and Ashford in Co. Wicklow after he had been in Dunganstown for 20 odd years so he was obviously well thought of within the church hierarchy too. Incidentally, I remember that one of Canon Foster's sons had rowed in the University Boat Race for Oxford and the oar of the boat was kept as a souvenir by Reverend Foster in the hallway of the rectory in Dunganstown.

The next family to take up residence in the rectory was the Burkes. Reverend Burke was totally different from Canon Foster, he came across as a pompous ass right from the start. He was an obnoxious sort of person who seemed to believe that he was God and that no one else counted. He started making changes very early on in his reign at the old rectory and he had some of the wonderful sweet chestnut and beech trees cut down. When these trees were felled I used my homemade cart for pulling the logs back to the old school house. The wheels were forever collapsing with the weight so I ended up using up all the wheels that I had salvaged – but it kept us warm for the winter and made my never-ending job of collecting firewood a lot easier.

To demonstrate his pomposity and general thoughtlessness, I recall the put-down he gave me when I showed interest in his new NSU car. As I was looking enviously at the new motor he astounded me by asking if I was going to buy one. Of course, I was very conscious of the fact that I could not afford to buy even a decent meal, never mind a car, and he knew this too. It was a very tactless comment on his part and to me very hurtful. I would have expected better from someone who wore the collar. I used do some jobs for him at his church and would attend evening services there. On one of these occasions he had an overseas missionary preacher with him and I remember the missionary worker asking, 'where does the young lad live?' Reverend Burke replied 'Oh, he lives at Dunganstown.' The young missionary worker looked puzzled and asked, 'How's he getting there?' to which the reply was curt and straight to the point, 'He's walking.' The overseas missionary worker quickly replied without thinking, 'Surely we could take him.' So, Reverend Burke was volunteered and forced into a job that he had no desire to do. He very reluctantly gave me a lift home. I could tell that it wasn't something that he was happy about doing and I suppose that I would have been considered to be too ragged and too smelly for his lovely new car.

On the journey it somehow came up in the conversation about all the different religions in the world. I suppose that I butted into their conversation as a young unbroken-in youth might do. I asked them why there were so many different religions and explained that I thought that if there weren't so many there might be more peace in the world. He replied to me very firmly that there was no need for all the other religions as he felt the Church of Ireland was more than capable of doing the whole job. He just made it very clear that there was no need for any religions other than his. He was quite capable of dealing with it all himself. Needless to say, he did not manage to convince me that he was right. I felt that he was being very arrogant in coming to his conclusion as he was not being tolerant and understanding of other people's feelings and views but that was what I had come to expect from him and on that trip I feel that I got to know him for who he really was.

I could sense at a very early age that Mr Burke and myself would not get on very well together. I recall one day when he was taking us to some function or another and he very rudely, and with pure arrogance, put me down – succeeding in totally belittling me. I, however, being only a child, often had to put up with such treatment, without complaint. I found him to be a very arrogant, uncaring, unsympathetic person and why he ever became a vicar was beyond me, but that was the way it was. You don't always have the right people doing the right job. In total contrast to her husband, Mrs Burke was a very pleasant and caring person. I used to do odd jobs around the garden for her and she would make me some lovely meals. She would pay me a few bob too, which came in very useful. She was obviously more aware our plight than a lot of people around us. While we were at Dunganstown she sometimes had a jug of soup sent for us kids to have in the winter period. This was very tasty and wholesome as she made her soup with the best ingredients that could be got at that time. It was a lifesaver to us during those cold long months.

Despite my opinion of Reverend Burke, I was never too far away from church activities and, it's odd, but even today I have to say that although I'm no longer a religious person I do enjoy the chance of attending the Church of Ireland's services. I find them very plain and straightforward and if you are lucky enough to find a clergyman that has got into the spirit of things it can be a very pleasant hour to spend. Every Sunday morning I would be at the church carrying out my duties dressed in rags and everyone else would be in their very smart Sunday gear. I remember that their shoes were so shiny you could see your face well enough even to shave in them. Of course, polish was not a thing that I ever troubled too much with in those days. Our family's poverty never caused anyone in the church any concern. They never seemed bothered to help us out of our pitiful situation. There were of course many ordinary people in that church who would also have found it difficult to exist from one day to another but the extremely rich people at that church (who did an awful lot for international charities and also in different parts of Ireland and collected regularly at their own functions) didn't seem to notice. They put a great deal of effort into their charities but it never seemed to dawn on them that there were plenty of people on their own doorstep who needed help.

I soon learned to avoid Reverend Burke. I would sneak off any evening that I ever had the chance to have a game of hurling on the practice field at Barndarrig and would stay there until it was dark. As this was a Catholic Club this was frowned upon but worse than that, I would join them after the Sunday morning service. This was certainly not an acceptable practice in the eyes of the Church of Ireland. We were not to play games of any sort on the Lord's day. When I was making my way back home after a Sunday game, I would be very mindful that the Reverend Burke would be coming back from Kilcandra. I was often walking up the long slope of Cavan's Hill and would see a glimpse of his car coming around at the bottom of the road. I then had to toss my hurling stick over the hedge till he had gone by. He would have gone mad at me if he had known that I had been playing a game of hurling on a Sunday morning. When I look back at it I can see that he had some very peculiar priorities. If he had cared as much about what was not right in my life i.e. my being hungry and with no decent clothes to wear and totally uneducated, his pompous attitude could have been put to far better use. It is strange but it has taken me a life-time going through life's university to make me realise that men like him did not do me any favours.

When the Reverend Burke moved on, we had a new young vicar by the name of Baird who really had his priorities sorted out and his heart in the right place. Sadly for me this was just a bit too late. I had very little to do with him or the church by this time and this was a disaster for my life. He quickly observed what all of his parishioners should have noticed about my hopeless situation. It was immediately very clear to him that the farm labouring I was doing would mean that I would have been a slave for the rest of my life. I'm sure that his opinion had nothing to do with the fact that I was working for a Catholic farmer. No, for Reverend Baird it was purely his concern for me and for my position. He suggested to me that I should consider joining a tank regiment in the UK where I might get the chance to get some education to give me a better chance in life. I suppose to be fair to him he did not know the full extent of my hopelessness and he went ahead and arranged for me to attend an army recruitment office in Belfast. I had an interview with a view to joining up, but of course in the late fifties Great Britain was not involved in any world wars so they were able to be more choosy.

I travelled to the recruiting office in a taxi.

The driver wanted to know where I was going, and I said, quite innocently and openly that I was thinking of joining the army. He looked at me very sternly and said 'You need to be very careful giving that type of information out up here. You could have a bullet put in your head before you start; this isn't rural Wicklow. Up here,' he continued, 'you need to catch yourself on very quickly'. After his outburst I puzzled over what I could have said that had revved him up so much and I wished I hadn't answered his question. You see, down our way nobody seemed to get so excited about these types of matters. I would hear on the radio about incidents and sometimes see it in the papers about 'orange boxes' getting blown up on the border. In my ignorance, I used to wonder what were they doing with all these oranges but my experience of going to Belfast for the day demonstrated to me just how different it was in the two parts of the country. I had no previous experience of dealing with diehard Unionists or diehard Republicans and this was a very serious wakeup call for me. I felt that it was like lifting a curtain and walking into a mad house. I found it very sad, that people from the six counties seemed to wind themselves up to such pitch. However my visit to the recruitment office was to turn out just as sad as they gave me some exams to do and I had no idea what they were about. They tried to encourage me and did seem very keen for me to join up. They gave me some papers explaining how I could arrive at the right answers and suggested I come back in six months time. They also sent me all of the travel warrants and refreshment vouchers for my day out. On the way back I bought a few firework bangers, as we did not have them south of the border. As we went over the border I felt as though I was carrying the haul from a bank robbery so I was very nervous in case I was checked. What I didn't realise at the time was that coming south they were not as bothered about people as they were about people going north. This experience – along with my fear of the exams – dampened the idea about going back in six months' time as I had been requested to and I never did go back.

The holy man who made the greatest impact on me, however, was not a vicar of the Church of Ireland, but a Catholic priest. It was Father John (Jack) Hans who ran the Marian Boxing Club in Wicklow. He and a committee of local people that he had got together, renovated and redecorated the ground floor of a derelict school building so that he could use it to found a club for the teenage boys of the parish. They worked hard through the winter of 1954 and the spring of 1955 and opened in March 1955. It is a credit to Father Hans' organising ability and tenacity that he managed to complete the task and so a very successful community facility came into being. It catered for boys between the ages of fourteen and eighteen who had left school and needed something to do in the evenings. The Club played a big part on the Amateur Boxing scene in Co. Wicklow and also provided opportunities for boys to play snooker, table tennis and board games as well as running Association Football and Gaelic Football teams.

Of course, this was a club for Catholic boys and, as I've said before this was a bit of a problem for me. I'm sure that my foster father can't have been aware that it was a Catholic club when he sent me there, as he did not normally expose me to such influences. To be fair Father Hans never once discussed whether I was interested in converting from my religion to his. I can tell you that this was a great relief to me because there were plenty of priests who would have no hesitation in trying to convert a young Protestant boy who was taking advantage of the Catholic facilities and obviously there were Church of Ireland clergymen who were just the same. I can only say that Father Hans to my way of thinking was not only a very good Christian but he also practiced it and he was a thorough gentleman.

So, my experiences with holy men during my childhood were mixed and, as a consequence, the influences and impressions that I retained vary considerably. While I can appreciate that church men like Father Hans and Reverend Baird had their hearts in the right place and were a positive influence on me, I also retained the awful impression that the majority were in the business for their own ends and could be thoughtless to the point of irresponsibility in their dealings with their parishioners.

Chapter 14

Escape to England

During the hopeless years after I left school and was working full time for a series of farmers, I never gave up dreaming of finding a better life. I don't want you to think that I was unhappy at this stage in my life because that was not the case. Though working from dawn till dusk for only my keep was very hard, I didn't mind hard work and, at least most of the time, I was better fed then than at any other time so far in my young life.

Nevertheless, despite the hard work, I had no money to spend on nights out like all the other young lads of my age had. I was aware that other lads enjoyed themselves together at weekends but the bit of money that I got apart from my keep went straight to my foster family. If I ever managed to get the money to go to a dance or to the pictures, it was a rare event and did not enable me to make the friends I so desperately needed. I wasn't able to build up a pattern. This left me in a world of my own with very few skills to help me integrate. I once went to a dance and plucked up the courage to ask a girl up to dance. I had no experience at this dancing business so I soon found myself in very deep water. We hadn't gone more than few steps before I began stepping on her toes. With a pained expression, she suggested that it might be better if we sat down and we did so with my face burning fit to start a fire. I suppose this poor girl saved a lot of girls of the future having their toes stamped on because I never, ever asked another girl to dance. I thought that there must be some other way of making friends with girls but, at that point, I was at a loss as to what exactly I should do – especially as I was usually short of funds.

In Ireland in those days every second house would have some kind of dance going on where there would be singing, piano accordion playing, tin whistles, flutes and in some cases a harp too. All of the people joining in at these impromptu events would have grown up being able to sing, dance and to play many of the musical instruments thus leaving them very competent people, able to mix easily in society. I couldn't play any sort of musical instrument as we had never owned any, I didn't know the words to the popular songs and I certainly couldn't dance. So you can imagine how far out of the normal society that I was.

The other thing that hindered my life and robbed me of any prospect of success – either with girls or in employment – was my lack of reading and writing skills. I had felt looked down upon at school and the teacher rarely paid me any attention and this, combined with the amount of time I took off to earn some money with my casual jobs, meant that my education was very limited indeed. This illiteracy was a continual embarrassment to me but I had no idea how to put the problem right or to improve my circumstances. The only solution seemed to be escape.

By this time, my foster sister Molly had left home and gone to live in England and it became my dream to do just the same. I used to get people to write to her to see if she could get me a place to stay where she was. Not one to let the grass grow under my feet, I had set about saving every penny that I could get. The letters were not having a great deal of affect and I hardly ever received a reply to them. I was to find out that she was more interested in what she could get out of me than in helping me to start a new life. I was very naïve and thought that she would do all in her power to help me – as I would have done for her. I suppose, knowing how the girl grew up and the appalling conditions she endured, I should have expected that this would have an effect on her character.

In fact, Molly had become a very wild girl before she ever went to England and this caused no end of problems at home. It would send my foster father mad trying to get her to come home at night at a sensible hour. I suppose that he left it too late to correct any problems with Molly but he often stood on the hill by the house roaring at her to get indoors. He was, of course, fearful of the consequences of her behaviour, especially as many of the people she associated with were much older than she was. By her teens she was well out of control and to make things worse she was a very nice looking teenager, which made it harder for him to deal with. His fears about her being in England on her own made him decide that he was going to go and join her as soon as he possibly could. His main problem was that he felt he couldn't live without the help of Daisy and May but he also couldn't live with them.

After church one Sunday morning he told me that he wasn't waiting any longer for Molly to get him somewhere to stay. He didn't think that she wanted him over there with her, so he eventually sent her a letter saying that he was going to come over and instructing her to make sure he had somewhere to stay. I was tremendously keen on this idea, of course, and asked him to let me know when he got any idea of when this was going to happen, as I would go with him. In the meantime I sorted out the references that Daisy told me I would need to make a good start in England. I got one from the police station, one from Daisy and one from the vicar. Funnily enough I was never asked for any of them when I got to England.

I kept saving and saving until I had the princely sum of ten pounds in my running away fund. The big day arrived and it was all or nothing. At the age of just eighteen, I was taking the biggest decision that I had ever made. I said my farewells to all and took a last lingering look around the home that I was leaving forever. My foster father and I made our way to Wicklow town and then caught the train to Dunlaoghaire. From there we caught the boat for England. I just hoped that I was doing the right thing.

When you think about leaving Ireland with only ten pounds to my name it may have seemed a bit rash. Some of my ten pounds I spent on my fares from Wicklow, the train fare, the boat fare from Holyhead and then the train fare to Rugby. Even in November 1960, that made a very big hole in my funds. I also had to pay for my keep, wherever I stayed. Running out of money was a big worry to me and I was very conscious that, for the first time since I left school at 13, I was unemployed and didn't know when I would next start to earn money. With only the clothes that I stood up in, I travelled light.

We arrived at Rugby station where Molly met us with her half-witted boyfriend, who had borrowed his grandfather's car to take us to Market Harborough where they were living at the time. Her poor old father's face was a picture when he set eyes on her boy-friend. He was less than amused when he met this boy but there was worse to come. As we were heading back towards Market Har-borough the boyfriend and Molly decided to give us a lesson in how they drove over here. We were flying along the roads that seemed so strange and busy to me, overtaking all of the cars that they came across in the boy-friend's grandfather's lovely little saloon. It was a Hillman car, which, apparently, was his pride and joy. By all accounts it took a great deal of persuading for him to lend the car in the first place. We approached a bad bend near Lubbenham and my foster father and me clung on. When we hit the bend the car spun out of control and turned over three times, narrowly missing a telegraph pole. It landed on its side so all we had to do was to climb out of the car in this position. We all stood by the car looking stunned and my poor old foster father leaned against the car in very severe shock wondering what the bloody hell had we let ourselves in for. As if all this wasn't enough, Molly's boyfriend pulled the car door down and as it came away it fell on my foster father's hand, breaking four fingers and leaving him with four very black nails. One of the cars that we had passed earlier in our insane journey arrived on the scene. The driver had a flask of rum, which he used to help the more severe victims of the crash. He looked almost as shocked as we were and said 'My God what were you trying to do? Could you not see the ice on the road?' He stated the obvious when he said 'It's a miracle that you got as far as you did, driving at the speeds you were doing. A wonder that you hadn't killed anyone.' It seemed to me that Molly's boyfriend would never wake up until he had destroyed either himself or someone else – he definitely wasn't very bright.

We gathered ourselves together and crossed over the road where two more Good Samaritan drivers had kindly offered to take us to the hospital. The grandfather's car was a write-off and you could imagine this didn't go down at all well. We all left the hospital and made our way to the grandfather's home. After the inevitable row about the car we found out to our horror that Molly had not discussed the living arrangements with her boyfriend's grandparents. She had led her father to believe that we were stopping with them so this was not a great start to this new adventure. A lot of very awkward discussions went on as to what was going to become of us and eventually the grandparents agreed that they would allow us to stay providing that we moved on fast.

I started looking for a job the very next day, but my foster father was unable to start any work for several months because of the injuries he had sustained in the crash. I felt that it was crisis time once again as it wasn't just a matter of me getting work for myself now but that I would have to keep my foster father as well until he was well enough to start work. I went looking at all of the local places around to see if I could get some work. I heard that at the council they had a vacancy for a road sweeper so I went along to see the man in charge. He told me that there was a job going all right but that he 'would not give it to a young lad like you. You should try and get an apprenticeship or a better job. You are far too young to start your life sweeping the roads.' This was not what I wanted to hear at this stage. This job would have been a job in clover after what I had been used to and being paid more money than I could have dreamt of. It just shows you that as right as the man might have been, he would have been far more charitable to me had he given me the job. I tried some of the local factories but I have to say my confidence of getting work couldn't have been lower and I wasn't getting any results. I would often be asked to fill out an application form. As soon as I saw the form I was gone like a shot because I couldn't fill it in. If they asked me questions about my education I knew it was pointless and one man even commented that he found the standard of my education quite unbeliev-able. Others who had vacancies wouldn't even consider me as they said that there was no point in giving me a job, as I would be called up for National Service soon. Things looked hopeless but when you are desperate you have to keep looking. I thought things had been hard in Ireland but at least at Callaghan's I was sure of my meal and a bed, but now all I'd had was a load of arguments and bad feeling because I was an unwanted guest with no work – and very unlikely to get any.

The grandparents' house in Market Harborough was on the main Leicester road – the A6. To me, after living in a quiet rural area this was like living in the middle of a racetrack with all the traffic tearing past. Not even in the night did it seem to let up, which meant that the first night in Market Harborough I couldn't sleep for a week! It was just one more thing about my new life that I would have to get used to.

After a great deal of hunting for work I found myself at an engineering factory where they made ornamental garden gates and also types of fuel storage and so on. To my amazement they didn't have any application forms to fill in and they didn't ask any prying questions as to whether I had been to school or not or whether if I were likely to be wheeled off to the army with barely a minute's notice. To me this was just heaven. I had wasted three days of my first week in England being cross-examined – and failing. To my enormous relief and delight the foreman said I could start on Thursday. He explained the type of work that I was expected to do – making bits for the gate on a jig for the welders to do their work on and then to dip the completed gate in big tanks of paint. By the end of the following week the foreman came to me and said that he was very pleased with my efforts and that he was going to have me trained up so that I could do the welding. I thought this was great and there were no hoops for me to jump through. But life doesn't ever seem to have gone very rosy for me and my next knock down was that the foreman's nephew turned up unexpectedly, looking for work. The foreman had him trained up instead of me and another opportunity had escaped me. There were plenty of advantages to this employment though. I was now earning money that I couldn't even have dreamt of before and they even paid me overtime rates. What's more they paid me without fail every week. When I consider the hours that I had worked on the farms, had I been paid for all those hours it wouldn't have taken me three years to save up for my trip to England. I could have bought the damned boat we travelled on! Things were not perfect however, as even with the money I was earning, after I had paid for my foster father and myself and sent a few bob over to Daisy to look after Sean, I did not have a great deal of money left.

By the time I was settled in to my job at the engineering factory, things were looking up despite any money worries I had. We had moved into comfortable digs and the landlady became fond of us and as she knew she was getting her few bob regular, she was happy to see us stay. My foster father's hand was getting better and we had picked out of the evening paper a job vacancy where there was a good chance for the three of us (that's my foster father, me and Molly's bigheaded boyfriend who's surname was Crackles so that's what we called him) to start earning more money than I was currently getting. So, we went to see the farm manager at the grass drying plant about twenty miles away. Crackles' grandparents were still spoiling him and they lent him the money to buy a three-wheeled van, which was an old Jowett Javelin. Well, we all got taken on and after about a week of our being there, an advert came on the television for cereals in which the characters were Snap, Crackle and Pop. From that point on that's what the three of us became known as.

Life wasn't just about earning a living but I still had problems in my life outside work caused by my lack of social skills and inability to read and write. I suffered a lot of teasing at the grass drying plant and was frequently the butt of practical jokes. I took particular exception to being called Paddy. I felt that I didn't have much given to me as a baby but that someone had seen fit to give me my own name – and it wasn't Paddy. Amongst all this teasing I did manage to make one good friend at the works – a lad called Smithy. He would take me to the occasional dance and to pubs in the area with the hope of getting me to like drinking beer but try as he may, he never made any progress in that area. We went to a dance one night in a village hall and all my old fears about socialising with girls resurfaced. Smithy tipped me off that this girl was interested in me and that I should go and see her. Well, we seemed to get on alright together but of course I didn't try any of that dancing business. I gave this girl a not-too-forward kiss for goodbye at the end of the evening but my mate Smithy went mad at me afterwards for not taking off my motorbike gloves before I kissed her! He took a very dim view of this and said that the girls would take an even worse view if I didn't change my habits. There you go, you're having to learn all of the time.

As I was to find out, Crackles was like my foster father in some ways; he did not like jobs that lasted too long. He had never done a twelve-hour shift in his life before the job at the grass drying plant so it wasn't too long before this work became difficult for him. More problems were to come. Daisy had been sending letters to us expressing her concern for Sean as he was supposed to be attending the Christian Brothers' school in Wicklow but, as she informed us, he was starting to run wild and had been playing truant. All these troubles seemed to land on my back, as I would always be very concerned on hearing this type of news. Knowing that my foster father was worried about the whole business, I eventually told him that I would send Sean's fare over.

Sean arrived and as he was not yet fifteen, it meant that he could not start a job, which did not amuse me, as I had started work at thirteen full-time. I could not see why his being a few months short of fifteen should make such a difference, but it was pointed out to me that this was England and not Ireland. So, although I was no longer having to pay for my foster father's keep for now, I was having to pay for my foster brother's keep, so I was no better off.

Molly had decided to have a quick wedding, which meant that it gave her father no chance to save up money to buy new clothes for the wedding and, of course, neither of us exactly approved of her choice of husband.

After the wedding, Molly and her family were a serious nightmare for me that ran on and on with no ending ever in sight. This nightmare was made worse because I was haunted by the thought of her children having to endure such terrible conditions so early in their life. I remembered the total lack of care that we got as children and I could not stand the idea of any other children in our family suffering unnecessarily. Their father seemed to become more incompetent and inconsiderate of their needs every day. While Molly and Crackles were together life was nothing short of hell itself and in the end the marriage completely broke up and I thought that maybe she would be able to put her life on a more even keel without him. Life though is never that simple and as it turned out the children were taken from her and then temporarily returned, which was obviously very disruptive for them. In the end two of her children were taken permanently and it took several years for her to track them down with the help of some Christian organisations. These people worked tirelessly to get them back for her and even provided Molly with accommodation for them all to live in. She did eventually manage to put her past behind her after finding a new man and they are still together to this day. Nobody can tell me that what she suffered in her childhood did not have a serious affect on her life. Until she was well on into her life, Molly had no idea how to look after herself and her children. Molly, however is one of these people who has come through the tunnel of no hope and would deny that she had ever entered the tunnel in the first place. She would only ever remember the happier things in her life, which I suppose is a good thing as there were not a lot of them to remember.

She certainly doesn't seem to want to remember that I ever gave her a penny or helped her in anyway whatsoever. I've always found this very baffling because if anyone ever did me a good turn I would never be happy unless I could find a way of paying them back. My foster sister and brother however, would show you no gratitude whatsoever for your efforts, whatever you did for them. They seemed to have that self-protective shell all around them to insulate themselves from anyone who might help them. I found, too, that they would often throw in my face that I was adopted and not their blood brother but when they needed help they would use the line, 'It's what a brother is meant to do'. The truth was that there never were any brotherly ties on their part except when I was wanted. Sean went on to become a multimillionaire though I can assure you he was not too particular about how he got there.

Having established myself in a decent job and digs in England, I felt proud of the new start that I had made, The problems of my adopted family never went away though and I wasted a lot of my early adult years worrying about them and trying to help them – financially and in a lot of other ways – but their inadequacies were something that I could not overcome and maybe I shouldn't have tried. I had my own life to lead and my own problems that still haunted me. I needed to know who I was and what my background was and until I sorted that out I could not rest.

Chapter 15

Finding out who I am

Although I settled down well in England and readily acknowledged that emigrating had been a good move for me, I still suffered problems because of my background and I was determined to find out more about my beginnings and my family. I was still haunted by the woman who used to follow me when I was about 4 years old, screaming for me to be given back to her. None of it made any sense to me. My lack of education and the stigma of my background left me feeling inadequate, with low self-esteem, as I always felt I wasn't like other people. I had grown up in an environment where there was no love and no care for me whatsoever. This blighted my whole life. When I got married I encountered great difficulties in things that would be normal to other people. These pressures have inevitably put strains on my wife and my children. I am very lucky to have the best wife in the world, as she has been very patient and understanding with me, and this has helped us through our lives.

I was starting from a point where I knew very little. I only knew that I was adopted. I was never told anything about why I was adopted or if I had a family. I didn't have any idea where my mother and father were – or even if they were still alive. Although I suspected that the woman who had followed me down the lanes of Dunganstown was my mother, I could only speculate about what had happened to drive her to the state she was in. Curiosity and the desire to find out who I really was were not the only reasons that drove me to make a concerted effort to uncover my background. I had been suffering with my health for many years and my consultants continually asked me if I had my medical records from my childhood, as they would assist them in diagnosing what was causing my problems. As I was a blank in this area – and many other areas – I could not assist them. In the absence of information, the medical people had had to carry out many procedures to assist them in diagnosing my blood problem. I worried constantly that my four beautiful daughters could possibly have inherited some awful health problem that I knew nothing about. I started trying to track down my roots in my twenties but it was to be a long and frustrating journey for me.

My first port of call for information about myself was the Bethany Home where I had been born and left behind by my mother. I tried repeatedly to get my records from the Church of Ireland Bethany home throughout most of my adult life but to say that they were not helpful would be a gross understatement. With the passing of the Freedom of Information Act, the Home Authorities have had to relent somewhat with some of my records, which I got in my sixtieth year [1999]. Unfortunately some of these records were released too late to assist me with my medical problems. So you can see these people have no concern whatsoever for people like me who were in their care. They didn't go out of their way to offer even the most basic of information. As one of the social workers for PACT (which now is the agent for the Bethany home), advised me, there was no need for records people like me as we had no value, nor were we of any interest to anyone. She asserted that that was the attitude of the people who ran these types of institutions. Appalling as this seems to me now, the Irish government aided and abetted them with this ploy, as the government officials did not carry out their duty to children like me. They failed in their responsibility to ensure that we were raised in civilized human conditions and that the care was of an acceptable standard and then they failed me again when I asked for information.

Eventually I overcame some of my social problems and was lucky enough to find myself a lovely, and loving, wife. Carol and I got married on the 25th March 1967 and she has always been a great help to me in trying to trace my real mother. As we'd been trying to carry out our search from the UK without finding out anything that could lead me to the whereabouts of my birth mother, we decided to go to Ireland to see my adopted father and Aunt May and we would continue with our search while we were there. As I had no idea where my mother came from this was obviously a very difficult task.

I had recalled a few places that I had overheard some people talk about when they were discussing this matter between themselves as is the way with 'adult matters' when they think that the children cannot hear them. One place was Ardee and another place that I had heard mentioned was Cavan but as Ardee was closest to us at the time we headed for there. We went to all the likely places where we thought that we could get the information that we needed, but we drew blanks everywhere we went. We were just about to give up our search when we thought we would try one last pub that we found. We asked the landlord the questions we'd asked so many others – 'Did he know anything about the Leinster family?' His answer was the usual 'No', but as we were about to leave he called us back and suggested that a family up the street by the name of Hargreave used to be friends of the Leinsters so they might be able to help. He thought that they may have been some sort of cousins but as it was many years since they had all left the area it was a slim chance. Well, we went to the address he gave us and a pleasant-looking lady opened the door. We told her what we were about but, as with all questions of this nature asked in Ireland, we got a very cautious, thought-out reply. However, our luck was about to turn, as an old aunt in the back room had overheard the conversation and she joined us at the door.

The old lady told the younger woman that she thought that I had every right to know who my mother was and where she was living today. Carol and I stood on the doorstep and stared, open-mouthed, unable to believe that we had finally found someone to help us. They invited us into their house and very quickly conjured up a pot of tea and some cakes. The old lady rushed around picking out photographs from various photo albums to make sure that we had a good range of snaps of the family that I had never known. This included a photograph of my mother on her wedding day to an RAF officer. It is very hard to describe what your feelings are when you are looking at a photograph of your real blood mother for the very first time. You have had your dreams and your daydreaming, your imaginations of someone but you have no idea of what they look like, so it is a shock, to say the least.

Now that I was armed with this information you would think everything else would be easy but it never is, is it? You see, it was never my wish to break into my mother's life with having no regard to how that would impact on her situation, so that meant that I had to take careful steps from here on in. Amy Hargreave put us in touch with a friend of my mother's who acted as a go-between for us so that we avoided any awkwardness. Her friend made arrangements for my mother to ring me for the first time and it was so strange for me to hear an educated Irish accent on the phone and to know that that was my mother. This was the same posh voice of those well-to-do ladies that I grew up amongst and the ones that would be looking down on this poor wretch of a kid; it was very hard for me to get my head around this huge gap in cultures.

It was arranged that I would meet my birth mother for the first time in my adult life in London at Victoria Station. She described herself so that I would recognize her on the station. The whole experience was mad, surreal. There were all those people rushing about trying to catch their train to wherever they were going and me trying to look for a lady that I didn't know, with only an old photo to help me. There were so many people hanging about, some looking a bit lost. It made me go through agonies wondering would it be this one or maybe that one. I worried about approaching the wrong woman. How could I say 'Hey, are you my mother?' People would think I was mad. But it is strange, when you have a meeting like this, as soon as your eyes fall on the person that you have an appointment with, there seems to be an inner connection to convince you that you have spotted the person that you have been so desperately wanting to find. The shock of that first meeting was tremendous and I think maybe that meeting should be very brief so that you can take in the enormous shock to your system. You're not really in any fit state to discuss all the things you want to. It would appear from my mother's point of view that she would have been quite happy just to see me and then to say goodbye but of course from my side there are all those questions that I have been desperately trying to find the answers for.

Carol and I went to have a look around Madame Tussaud's with my mother and then she took us to a restaurant to have a cup of tea and a chocolate biscuit. Eventually, it was down to the very thorny issue that I had waited all this time and travelled all this way for. Her reaction to my questions was very calm and composed. She went into some depth as to why I was abandoned and all of the reasons that she gave me then pointed to it being other members of her family who had caused this to happen, which left me feeling that she was the victim of circumstances just as I was. She gave me her age as being sixteen when she gave birth to me, which, I was to find out much later, was not correct.

Despite her calm exterior, I knew that this must have been a very stressful experience for my mother. The decision she took in her teens would have been a very heavy load to have to carry and now she was face to face with her past. After we had talked for some time, she excused herself and went to the ladies' powder room. She had been gone a few minutes and Carol got worried so she followed her. It was obvious that my mother was overcome with emotion and she gave Carol an engagement ring to mark the occasion.

As we parted, she assured me that she would keep in touch but, as her second husband wasn't aware of my existence nor were her two teenage daughters (my half sisters), we would all have to be discreet. I had to keep a low profile until her daughters were older. It was obvious that my mother did not want them to have any reason to believe that their mother wasn't able to practice what she might want to preach. I found it sad that she said how sorry she was that I had not found her before she had got married for the second time as she admitted that she may not have got married if she had met me.

Several months after that meeting in London I contacted my mother again via our go-between but she informed me that she did not want me to communicate with her again as she had found the whole situation far too painful. As she could not put the clock back she could find no reason why she would want to keep in touch with me. This was devastating to me. I still had so many unanswered questions. She hadn't even told me who my father was. But the most hurtful thing was realising that she hadn't wanted me as a baby and she didn't want to know me now – at 27 years old. Despite this seemingly callous behaviour, I am still trying to find excuses for my mother's actions all those years ago.

Some time later, we heard from Amy Hargreave that my mother's husband had died suddenly. By coincidence, we were going on holiday to Weymouth which wasn't too far from my mother's place in Dorset so we thought it might be a good idea if we called on her. Surely this could not cause the same problems that it may have caused in the past. I was determined to get answers to my questions so we did not give her advance notice of our visit. Carol and I arrived at her home on a beautiful summer's

Sunday morning. There was a girl in her late teens in the garden and after we had eyed one another warily for a few seconds, I asked her if Mrs Crocker was at home. She replied, in a pleasant, refined accent, that her mother was not yet back from church but she would be back any minute. She offered me an orange drink with ice and, noticing Carol in the car with the kids, she offered them refreshments too.

As we all finished the drinks, standing around in the beautiful garden, my mother arrived back from church. She saw Carol first and went straight over to her, smiling and asking politely how she was, then she got around to inquiring who she might be. When Carol replied that she was Derek's wife, my mother's manner changed completely. Her face became ashen and she was suddenly very agitated – jumping about as if somebody had put a bucketful of ants in her knickers! She then saw me chatting to her daughter, Alison, and curtly instructed her to go inside to fetch something out of the house. With Alison out of the way, she then dealt with us. She made it very clear that today it would not be possible to visit with her at all but she did invite us to come back in the middle of the week when she would serve us dinner. We were all then gathered up and ushered very hastily towards our car.

As we drove back down her long driveway to the main road, we noticed her estate's graveyard and small chapel. We stopped and had a quick look around this interesting building and I must admit that I pondered the importance of the situation of the family members buried there compared with mine.

We came back as agreed a few days later and we all spent the day by the sea. At first you could see that my mother was doing all she could to keep a distance between herself and me and my children – her grandchildren. It was as if she was in a large block of ice and as the sun became warmer you could see the ice dripping away and it was getting thinner as the day progressed. It was as though she was having a huge battle within her soul as to whether she should continue with her resistance or whether she should let go the struggle and accept things so that she could open her arms and welcome her grandchildren and her son into her heart. We arrived back at her place and went into her best room where all of her beautiful dinner service with silver cutlery was put out for our use for the meal that she was about to serve. She certainly took great pride in entertaining her guests. And I was to find out much later what a reputation she had for being a great hostess.

In response to my questions, she set out to give me the answers I had been searching for. She informed me that she became pregnant at the age of 15 and I was born when she was 16 and that she had been unaware that she was pregnant till she was almost in labour. She maintained that she had no part to play in my being given up for adoption as she was sent to England to finish her education. Her family had told her that her baby would be fostered out until she was old enough to sort things out. But, of course, when she came back from England she learned that a family who her family were not able to identify had adopted me. I was lost to her. She gave very little information on all of the other matters that I was desperate to find out about. She felt able to explain her part in my beginnings but she refused to give me any information on my father whatsoever. I found it very difficult to believe her lack of cooperation in this matter but I did feel a great sadness for her plight regarding my birth and the circumstances surrounding it.

I could see that I was not going to make any further progress at this meeting. I think it was worthwhile to have had this meeting though, because at least she was able to see her four grandchildren. I hoped that despite what I had missed with her, she might be able to enjoy her grandchildren. They were beautiful children and any grandmother would have been very proud and honoured to have them as their granddaughters. On leaving we had a brief but emotional, private conversation. I said 'Although you didn't look after me as a child I have always had a great sense of love for you.' She was amazed by this and said 'No, you haven't. How could you? How could you?' It didn't matter what I said to her she was having none of it and this mystified me, but of course at that time I didn't know what I was to find out twenty years later, which was to make the picture a lot clearer. She knew that not only had she abandoned me as a baby but also that she had been lying to me now that I was a young man. I would be well into middle age before I realised just how guilty she was.

We hoped to visit Amy the next time we were in County Wicklow as she had become, by now, a very special friend. She pleaded with us to make it soon as she had something to discuss with me and really needed to see my family and me but, before we could make the trip to Ireland, she passed away. I was always grateful that somebody like her suddenly came into my life and wanted to make me part of her family. I was never to find out what she was so desperately wanted to see me about on that occasion. I had noticed a dramatic change in Amy during the months immediately before her death. When I had first contacted her, she was cautious but she gradually changed to become very co-operative and helpful to me in my search. But then, suddenly, she was worried and desperately wanted to see me. It is frustrating to think of all the chasing around that I have done in trying to find people who were associated to my family's roots and I always found the doors locked and bolted and there was never anybody willing or able to give me any information and yet when I had overcome all of these barriers to find this lovely lady, that it was swiped from under my nose. I will always remember Amy, who put justice before family secrets for no gain for herself – just to help me.

I had many more phone conversations with my mother in the years following that second meeting. She would never ring me – I would always have to ring her and I must confess that her lack of interest and effort upset me. Eventually, she told me who my father was but he had passed on some years before, so meeting my father was impossible. I am certain that she purposely kept his identity from me until it was too late and she then had the insensitivity to make me aware that my father had expressed to her that he wanted to see me before he died. It makes me unbelievably sad to think that she denied both him and me the chance to know one another.

The PACT records confirmed some things that my mother had told me – for example, that when my mother said that she was in no position to bring up a child and would have had no means of keeping me (unless she had help from her well-to-do family, of course), she was right, but the records clearly show that her date of birth does not tally with the lies that she had convinced me into believing. In every conversation I ever had with my mother she had blamed her mother for having to leave me in the Bethany Home. She said that she hadn't been in Ireland when the fostering arrangements took place and that she had been in England completing her education. I learned, many years after my meetings with my mother, that she had actually been in the room when the documents were signed. Had I not had access to the records of my birth and fostering, I would never have known the truth, so why should these people deny people like me this access. If my mother had told me the truth when I met her for the first time I would not have liked it, but I would have been able to respect her more for telling me the truth rather than me having to live my life with nothing but lies. It might also have made things easier for her because, had I known the truth, I would not have wished to keep in touch with her except to get the details about my father. I would have left her to stew in her own sad life of shame and misplaced pompousness in which she was so good at shrouding herself in her world, where it is important for the right image to prevail. She had obviously found it easier, even as a young woman, to pretend that everything was going to be OK and to ignore problems that faced her. She seems to have passed her responsibilities on to an organisation and, to her, it was inconceivable that these arrangements could be anything but wonderful for the unwanted child. You would have to be very single-minded never to question the possibility that so called 'good organisations' would ever fall down on the care of the child that you had walked away from. Perhaps, also, the people who ran these homes must shoulder some blame in relation to my mother, as I'm sure they did not tell her the truth about how they would treat me. My mother certainly wasn't all bad, as she raised her first daughter from her first marriage as good as any mother could have done and she made sure that she had a first class education. She had an even more difficult task with her daughter from her second marriage as she was born with Down's syndrome. She was steadfast in her support of that child. She was just never a mother to me.

Another question that I was so keen to get answered by my birth mother was 'Was she the woman who used to follow me when I was with my foster mother, screaming for me to be given back to her?' The answer was no, so I drew a blank there and the mystery remained. The next track that I decided to follow was that of the family with whom I was fostered out at seven and a half months in Nun's Cross, County Wicklow. I assumed that there was a strong possibility that this lady might have been the one who followed me all those years ago. I needed the name of the family who I had lived with at that time but the PACT records people were adamant that they would not reveal it to me. We wrote many letters and made many phone calls to try to persuade them to give me this information and you can never imagine how frustrating it was to get so close to being able to resolve a mystery which has shrouded your life for over 50 years, I suggested to them that if the lady who fostered me had passed away then they could get in touch with her next of kin and ask them would they mind me getting in touch with them. This seemed a sensible suggestion to me, and one that would be unlikely to cause any hurt or inconvenience but you would not believe that these people could be so awkward. This seemed like my last chance to unravel this mystery and in the end they were very reluctant in doing as I requested. In the end they found that Mrs Shirley's son – for Mrs Shirley was indeed the lady who had followed me all those years ago – was desperately keen for me to make contact with him. The funny thing is that these people did everything in their power to persuade him not to contact me and to leave things as they were as this would be 'best for all'. But they hadn't reckoned on how important it was to old Tom, Mrs Shirley's son, and he demanded that he was given the full particulars of how he could get in touch with me. Sometimes, you don't give any thought to the fact that the people you wish to find, often want to find you as much as you want to find them. I had a wonderful meeting with Tom and he filled in many of the gaps in my knowledge of what happened to me as a very young child. He told me about how he used to play with me in the old wheelbarrow, where he would take me and about the other children in the family – things that, under normal circumstances, parents or siblings would have told me as I grew up.

While I was in Ireland to see Tom, I went back to Daisy and May's old place on the hill and was amazed at how things had changed. A Dublin builder had bought the place from my foster brother, Sean, at a price that was convenient for a very quick sale. He had turned the whole place into a mansion and built new stables for horses. He had also bought a great deal of additional land that surrounded the old farm. He bought Conway's old farm, and some of the Williams's fields and now it is a very fine place. I've been back a few times to see the area and once I ended up going up onto the old place and the memories all came flooding back. It was as though I was a lonely little boy again out there on the hills with the goats. The memories of being cold and hungry were there, the memories of having my finger trapped in the rabbit trap, the memories of carrying huge loads of timber on my back from all over the place to try and keep a fire going. In the main, they were not pleasant memories.

I had started looking for answers in my twenties as to why I had been placed in that position and now, here I was, a man in middle age with explanations of why I had been abandoned, why I had been mistreated, why I was so neglected that I became ill and grew up not being able to read and write. But although I've now gathered some of the facts surrounding my birth, around the fostering arrangements and about my childhood, I still don't understand it all. I still don't know how some of the players in this sorry show – my mother and her family, the people in charge of the Bethany Home, the Church of Ireland authorities, the Irish Government, the neighbours living alongside me in the community – can live with themselves and why they thought their behaviour could possibly be acceptable. But my fight goes on. Having got the information, I have fought long and hard to get the injustice of my treatment recognised by the authorities. So far, the Irish Government has not included the Bethany Home in the terms of their Redress Bill. This would be admitting that things were not right there and would probably bring other Church of Ireland homes into the frame. There are now questions being asked in high places as to why so very few Church of Ireland institutions have been included in the Redress list and I will keep pressing for answers. I will be looking for an admission that wrong was done. I also want to make sure that children can never again be treated in this careless, cavalier way.

When you go into all of this you find that the churches and the governments are the real causes of their people behaving in such an inhuman fashion. People are made to feel ashamed and they fear the loss of face, the loss of their family pride. But of course, there is no shame in having children whether married or unmarried – that shame is a man-made illusion. Where there is shame, real shame, is having children that you dump on someone else to look after, pushing away your responsibilities. If people had not been made to feel – by the churches and the government – that this was acceptable behaviour then thousands of people would have been saved injustice and suffering. Children were made to endure this just so that their parents and the rest of society could pretend to the world that they are leading examples, with not a blemish on their soul. Simply to save face they put things in the back of their minds. But in this pretend society there are no winners because both sides are the real victims, the child, the mother (and sometimes the fathers as well) as their families will always have their hidden shame.

Chapter 16

And who am I?

Despite my poor beginnings and the disadvantages I brought with me from my childhood – not being able to read and write, not knowing how to behave in social situations, the poverty and the attitudes to money, food and authority, I have found more contentment in my life now that I have found out my roots. I'm married to a wonderful woman – and have been for many years. We have four beautiful daughters who have all made me proud in their own ways and grandchildren who are helping us to have fun now that we are in our later years. I worked all my life from leaving school at thirteen years old and made more of a success of it than might have been expected when I was a poor young lad in Ireland or when I first came to England with no skills at eighteen.

So, what's changed in the last forty or so years since I was a scared, but excited young man getting off the boat in Holyhead? I would have to answer that question by saying 'Almost everything'. I am now far more confident and can function in many social situations. I'm happy and I'm well fed. I have adequate clothing (including those elusive long trousers, of course!) and plenty of other possessions – although material things have never held the same attraction for me as they seem to have for many other people. Best of all though, is that I now have people who love and care for me. In complete contrast to my childhood, I feel that the family that I have created for myself really cares. Never again need I fear someone saying that I am not wanted and that I could be sent back to where I came from. The security and peace of mind this gives me is something that many people may find hard to understand – but it is very real to me. What has not changed is my frustration at not knowing enough about my background and my desire to get answers.

As I get older I can look back with forgiveness and understanding – but not in all areas of my life. I can forgive people like my foster father and mother. They had their own problems and neither had had a good start in their own lives. As I've said before, they were not bad people; they were just unable to cope and really should not have been given the extra responsibility that they took on when they fostered me. They didn't know that they were doing wrong – but the people in authority who made the arrangements must have known that the situation was far from ideal. I had even managed to forgive my mother until I found out about the lies she told to protect herself. She had a childhood blessed with everything anyone could ever have wanted but she didn't seem to appreciate the importance of that opportunity for me and certainly did not consider giving me the benefit of an upbringing in similar circumstances. Of course, the reason she was so thoughtless towards me was that she was just thinking about herself and about her family. Their good name and their pride were more important than the baby she had brought into the world so she abandoned me to a life of poverty and hardship and that I find very difficult to understand. It makes me sad to think she didn't want me and that she allowed bigotry to dictate the course of my life. And after all that, when I found her she lied. She lied to protect her new family, her privileged position and above all, to protect her view of herself. Even faced with the son in his twenties that she had given up as a baby and who was searching for answers to questions he had been asking all his life, she could not tell the truth. The things she told me were things that did not disturb her opinion that she had done nothing wrong and which justified her actions to me and to herself. If a woman of her age in that situation cannot be honest with herself, then something deep is going on and I am unable to understand the logic of it. What I eventually discovered was that, far from being out of the country when my adoption took place, she was actually a signatory to it and, rather than being a young teenager at the time, she had been a woman over 21.

Never one to bear a grudge, my wife Carol has regularly sent Christmas cards to my mother and her family and also news of her grandchildren and great-grandchildren but we have had no response in over twenty years. I feel sad for her in this respect – she doesn't seem to know what she is missing. Of course, my daughters and grandchildren have asked questions about their grandmother and great-grandmother but I am unable to give them the detailed answers they need so the mystery carries on through the generations.

In my unending search for answers I managed to meet with some of my mother's and father's families. Finding them was far from easy, especially as my father had died some years before. You really can't go and knock on a door and say 'Hello, your father was my father.' Just imagine the shock and upset this could cause. The thought that I would never see, hear, touch or speak with my real father was always with me and it saddened me that, because my mother had delayed giving me the information, I had missed the opportunity to get to know him. It seems even more difficult when you think that some years before his death I had re-fuelled my car in my father's garage in Drumconrath and didn't have a clue that the garage owner was in fact my very own father.

On one of our many trips to Ireland, one of the neighbours in Drumconrath village suggested that I go to see old Mr Flannery who had worked for my grandfather and his half brother in County Dublin. When we went into this old gentleman's house it was as if he had seen a ghost. He started rubbing his face saying 'This is incredible. After all these years!' He could not believe that the likeness of my father and myself could be so profound. He was one of the very few people who not only knew that a baby had been born but also that I was a boy. He also knew my mother very well from her frequent visits to my father's garage.

Eventually, the neighbours told me in a coded way that there could be no doubt that Jim Doyle was my father and said that I should go to see Andy who would be my half brother. When you see him, they told us, you won't have any doubt who is your half brother. We didn't contact him straight-away but contacted the Social Services in Rugby who gave us the name of one of the surviving members of my father's family. We met her and she agreed to address a letter to Andy with her phone number, for his use, to save embarrassment all round if he didn't want any contact. She informed me that there had been ten children in the family but only seven surviving – two girls and five boys. It was mind boggling to think that I have two half sisters and five half brothers when just a couple of years before this breakthrough I did not know that any of these existed. It was like someone had pulled the curtains on a stage wide open.

It turned out that Andy couldn't wait for us to go over to see him but his mother was not very well so we put off going over for a week or two for her to make some recovery. We got a message from Andy that his mother was making good progress and for us to come on over, so off we went. When we got to Andy's home everywhere was closed up. I immediately started to think that he had changed his mind and was avoiding me but, after asking around, I was relieved to find him at the house next door. Bad news greeted me though. Andy's mother had passed away the night before. I felt sick to the bottom of my stomach. The last thing these poor people needed was for a half brother to turn up at this point. However, Andy was a pillar of strength and went over to the car where my wife and my daughter were waiting to see the likeness and wondering how it was all going. He insisted that he wanted us to meet all of his sisters and brothers no matter what, and even invited us to go to the funeral but I could not agree that it would have been appropriate for us to attend.

We arranged to meet at a hotel the day after the funeral and Carol was staggered to see the likeness between Andy and me. We had the same claw-like markings around the eyes and our hands were identical. Some brothers didn't look like Andy or like me but with some of the others there was no disputing that I was the son of the same father. We spent a very informative night with Andy and he made it very clear that if my father had been told of my whereabouts when I was a child he would have got into his big Singer car to fetch me, irrespective of who it might have displeased. This is knowledge that I treasure but, deep down, I know this could never have happened – my mother would not have allowed it. The gap between Protestants and Catholics was just too wide.

One piece of information my mother gave me was that her maiden name had been Leinster (whereas I had always believed it to be Linster) and this led me to my grandparents. This was big progress for me so we decided that we would take another trip to Ireland to check out the family name of Leinster in Co Cavan. But first we did a bit of research in this country. A business contact had connections in County Cavan and told me that the name Leinster was often spelled Linster. Confirmation of this came when we met and became friendly with a family of Linster's in Wiltshire who had the same desire to check out the roots of their name. Leslie Linster had found out some history from his many years of probing. He discovered that going back to his grandfather's time his family were known as the Leinsters but when they left the police in Ulster to join the English police some of them changed their name to Linster. So now I had two names to investigate. Unfortunately it is not easy for Church of Ireland family names to be traced, as the main records office was burnt down during the troubles of 1916.

While we were over in Ireland we called in to see some of my mother's family – the Leinsters (we had been in contact with each other by letter and phone on a regular basis prior to going). We couldn't have met nicer people. Florence Leinster has worked tirelessly on my behalf in trying to sort out all of the unanswered questions that have been part of my life for as long as I can remember and I was extra grateful as she helped me despite not being a blood relative – just related by marriage. They made contact with some first cousins of my mother's for me – the Foy family and old Lilly McKeague. After several false starts caused by a variety of problems – Lily's ill health, the long journey to Wexford and even an accident suffered by my wife – we managed to meet up with Lily and the Foys. It was marvellous.

My wife and I met many relations on my mother's side and the funny thing is, every one of them flung their doors wide open to us. They discussed my background in a grown up manner and all of the rubbish, embarrassment and shame that I had become used to and which, of course, I half-expected from my mother's family never came into it. The only shame I found here was the shame they felt at having to accept that I had been denied a normal family environment and that my mother and her family hadn't been more concerned for my welfare rather than worrying about me being born outside of wedlock.

As I listened to this loving family telling me the truth about my family history, I came to the conclusion that there is no money in this world that could compensate for having lost the chance to have this in your childhood. Meeting my family was a wonderful experience that I wouldn't have missed for the world but it did make me realise more fully what I had missed. The real tragedy of my childhood wasn't just the poverty and the hunger or the lack of decent clothing, it was the total lack of love and affection. What I had really missed out on was having a family who cared.

I am still unable to understand or forgive the attitude of the authorities that I have met with in my long search for answers. They have been nothing short of obstructive in the majority of cases. Why do they think that people in my situation – adults who just want to know about their roots – should not be given all the help that it is possible for them to give? While I can appreciate that sometimes hurt may be caused by a missing child turning up out of the blue or someone raking up old, painful memories, I did not get the feeling that this was why many of the organisations that I approached for help did not want to assist me. No, mostly it seemed to me that they had other reasons for the obstacles they put in my way. Sometimes they were protecting their organisations or just doing something because 'it's always been done that way'. Sometimes, they did not have the information to give me – but rarely did I encounter a true desire to be helpful in these cases. All I met was a shrug of the shoulders and a complete lack of understanding of the problems that this caused me. Some even asked what I expected and seemed to think it was acceptable that people in my situation should be treated badly. Of course, I also met a precious few people who went out of their way to help me. Amy Hargreave was just one such person. As soon as she appreciated my problem, she did everything she could to welcome me and to assist me in my quest to find my mother and details about my family. I have had no professional help in my search or in coming to terms with my situation and until recently I didn't even know that there are organizations who can help people in my position. I think that even if I had known I would have been reluctant to seek help because I was still affected by my own inner shame.

My struggle with the authorities goes on. I am still striving to get justice from the Irish Government and while great strides forward have been made by the Catholic community, there is little or no help for Protestants affected by the Irish State's disgraceful policies during the 1940s and 1950s. Many Catholic institutions have been included in the Irish Government's Redress Bill that aims to ensure that the problems caused by abuse of children in care are recognised and to compensate these people for their suffering. To date very few, if any, Church of Ireland Mother and Baby Homes have been included in the list of institutions for which compensation cases can be heard. I was excluded from society in my childhood and am still being excluded today. The authorities refuse to listen but I continue to campaign.

So, how has my life turned out? With my lack of education and knowledge of the 'ways of the world', it could have been expected that I would find it difficult to find and keep a reasonable job, let alone be given any responsibility. This has not been the case. I worked hard as a young boy and I have since learned that what was expected of me then was far more onerous than anything that would be expected in a more conventional job in England. I've worked in a car plant, a grass-drying works, a tile works and in engineering and packing operations. I've worked for the council and in the construction industry. I've even had a go at starting my own construction business.

Carol always filled in application forms for me when necessary and on one occasion she did this for a job at Chrysler motor company in their packing section. This job doubled my wages from the start but, as it turned out, we weren't being paid the proper agreed union rate for the job. It wasn't long before I was elected shop steward for the plant and went on to be the convener for the union. I felt that at this point I had started to move with the big boys, which was a far cry from my younger years working for farmers. The people I was working with had a great deal more experience of the business and I had to learn fast. I tried to apply fairness with common sense as a non-negotiable aspect in my union dealings. I was coming up against people who had had proper educations and so I felt that I had to work hard to keep up. However, the majority of my workmates believed that I was not out of my depth when I was in negotiations. I've always had to rely on memory because of my lack of reading skills and, as I wasn't totally reliant on a piece of paper or a notebook, this could make even these clever people feel at a disadvantage. I could argue with conviction and calmness when I knew my case was right so I managed reasonably well.

I've been married for over thirty years to Carol and she is a wonderful wife, the best that God ever put on the Earth and the best mother that any child could have been lucky enough to have. She also became my right hand as she helped me with my union work and all the paperwork that went with it plus the administration that I got landed with from the boxing club. Without her help I would never have been able to carry on in these two fields. She is the main reason why I have been able to overcome the difficulties that the disadvantages of my early years caused.

One of the things from my childhood that I'm happy to say has continued is my love of boxing. I boxed for the Territorial Army (achieving several quarter-final places and even winning the tournament for my unit at different weights) and also for several boxing clubs in and around Rugby. When the first boxing club I had joined in England closed down I had to look around for another as by this time I couldn't imagine life without boxing. At the time there were lots of clubs – about twenty in Coventry alone – and many Irish lads who worked with me at the car plant were also involved with boxing. Eventually I moved on and I started my own boxing club in Newbold village near Rugby and achieved some good results, as well as getting a great deal of satisfaction and enjoyment from seeing the young lads increase in confidence just as I had done all those years ago in Ireland.

I am content that I have helped my foster family to the best of my ability. One way or another they have all caused me grief and worry and have cost me huge amounts of money. Their inability to support themselves from time to time has meant that they frequently relied on me to provide basic necessities and to dig them out of scrapes. Both Molly and Sean seemed to expect my help as of right and would have no compunction about taking my money even when it was obvious that I didn't really have much to spare. Molly seems to have the ability to forget any help she's received in just the same way as she blocks out all the bad things that have happened in her life and she will probably always have to struggle through life. Sean, on the other hand, took my help and money when he needed it but, even though he is now a very rich man, he does not feel that he should repay any of it. Having said that, I probably would not accept anything from him as I know that his fortune has been made at others' expense – and not necessarily honestly. Despite all this, I do not regret the help I gave as I feel that it was my duty to help my family if I could – even though they were not my blood family.

That's my story and it has been a story about shame. At the centre has been my mother, Hannah's shame when she abandoned me to avoid bringing shame and disgrace on her bigoted family. But it is also about the shame that the government and the Church of Ireland should feel that they ignored their responsibilities towards defenceless babies who were placed in their care. Above all it is about my continual shame. My growing up years are characterised by the feelings of shame I had – shame about how I looked, shame about the way I smelled, shame that my family didn't want me. This continued into my adult years when the feelings became more subtle but were just as real. I felt shame that I did not have the same social skills as 'normal' people and that I had to hide the fact that I could not read and write very well. When people with normal backgrounds discussed their families, I had to keep quiet. When my daughters asked questions about their grandparents, I was ashamed that I couldn't give them proper answers. Finding some of the answers to the questions that have plagued me all my life and finding relatives who care has finally relieved some of that shame for me.

Of course, this is just the tip of the iceberg of my life's experience but I hope you've been interested in taking this journey with me.

The publishers hope that this book has given you enjoyable reading. Large Print Books are especially designed to be as easy to see and hold as possible. If you wish a complete list of our books please ask at your local library or write directly to:

Magna Large Print Books
Magna House, Long Preston,
Skipton, North Yorkshire.
BD23 4ND

This Large Print Book, for people
who cannot read normal print,
is published under the auspices of

THE ULVERSCROFT FOUNDATION

... we hope you have enjoyed this book.
Please think for a moment about those
who have worse eyesight than you ...
and are unable to even read or enjoy
Large Print without great difficulty.

You can help them by sending a
donation, large or small, to:

**The Ulverscroft Foundation,
1, The Green, Bradgate Road,
Anstey, Leicestershire, LE7 7FU,
England.**
or request a copy of our brochure for
more details.

The Foundation will use all donations
to assist those people who are visually
impaired and need special attention
with medical research, diagnosis
and treatment.

Thank you very much for your help.